# EARTH RECITALS

*Essays on Image and Vision*

## OTHER BOOKS BY MELISSA KWASNY

### POETRY

*The Archival Birds* (Bear Star Press, 2000)
*Thistle* (Lost Horse Press, 2006)
*Reading Novalis in Montana* (Milkweed Editions, 2009)
*The Nine Senses* (Milkweed Editions, 2011)

### NOVELS

*Modern Daughters of the Outlaw West* (Spinsters Ink Books, 1990)
*Trees Call for What They Need* (Spinsters Ink Books, 1993)

Melissa Kwasny is also the editor of *Toward the Open Field: Poets on the Art of Poetry 1800–1950* (Wesleyan Poetry Series, 2004), and, with M.L. Smoker, the anthology *I Go to the Ruined Place: Contemporary Poems in Defense of Global Human Rights* (Lost Horse Press, 2009).

# EARTH RECITALS

*Essays on Image & Vision*

*by* Melissa Kwasny

Lynx House Press
Spokane, Washington

# ACKNOWLEDGMENTS

Grateful acknowledgment is given to the editors of the following journals and books where some of the essays first appeared in part or in full:

*26 (twenty-six):* "Learning to Speak with Them"
*American Poetry Review:* "God-Step at the Margins of Thought" and "Women and Nature"
*Cerise:* "The Flower Artist"
*Gettysburg Review: "Dov'è il Tevere"*
*Tracy Linder: Windswept.* Exhibition catalog, Holter Museum of Art, Helena, Montana.
*Pleiades:* "Conference of the Birds"
*West of 98: Living and Writing the New American West* (University of Texas Press): "The Imaginal Book of
    Cave Painting"

"Women and Nature" was presented, in an abbreviated version, during a panel under the same name, at the 2009 AWP Conference in Denver, Colorado. My gratitude to the other panelists, whose insights and luminous poems inform my work: Sarah Gridley, Janice N. Harrington, Rusty Morrison, and M.L. Smoker.

My gratitude also goes to the Montana Arts Council, which granted me an Artist's Innovation Award for work toward "The Imaginal Book of Cave Paintings."

A special thanks goes to Sara Scott, Montana archeologist, for her scholarship and expertise in my exploration of pictographs and petroglyphs.

This book would not have been written without the literary, intellectual, and imaginative guidance of my wise and generous friends and first readers: Bryher Herak, Robert Baker, and Rusty Morrison.

Thank you especially to the many writers and artists included herein whose work has guided me and which illuminates my practice and inspires this book.

*Cover art: Untitled* by Nan Parsons. Other fine paintings by Nan Parsons may be viewed at
    www.nanparsonsart.com
*Book & Cover Design by* Christine Holbert

LYNX HOUSE PRESS books are distributed by the University of Washington Press, 4333 Brooklyn Avenue NE, Seattle, WA 98195-9570

LIBRARY OF CONGRESS CATALOGING-IN-PUBLICATION DATA

Kwasny, Melissa, 1954-
[Essays. Selections]
Earth recitals : essays on image & vision / by Melissa Kwasny.
    pages cm
Includes bibliographical references.
ISBN 978-0-89924-128-9 (alk. paper)
1. Imagery (Psychology) in literature. 2. Imagery (Psychology) in art. 3. Symbolism in literature. 4. Symbolism in art. 5. Consciousness in literature. 6. Consciousness in art. I. Title. II. Title: Essays on image & vision. III. Title: Essays on image and vision.
PS3561.W447E23 2013
814'.54—dc23
                    2012042577

# TABLE OF CONTENTS

When I feed the birds, standing on the ladder beneath the tree with my bucket of seeds, the chickadees land on the branches around me. They are so delicate, their legs like black string tied around the thinnest limbs of the poplar, their tiny eyes focused on me, each move a heart-flutter closing in, coasting just past my hair or my hand—at least twenty of them. I feel gifted by their tameness. They are an other-life come close, trusting me, though it is true that I have earned their trust. I feed them suet and seeds. Chickadees live, on average, about three years, so this might be the sixth or seventh generation I am feeding. They create a halo around me, each lighting up, when they settle, as stars do, around a center star or sun. For one moment, I have become their center of gravity. In all their complexity, they extend the sphere I feel them make around me, "haphazard as in happiness and happen," as poet Sarah Gridley writes to me. They hover in place as my friends do, as my family does, now, momentarily, in this lifetime, creating an image of the sensate world that surrounds me before I, and all of them, vanish.

The image in literature is as ancient as the pastures in the Psalms, as the figures in Plato's cave, as the owl or bear in aboriginal song. Image: anything perceivable by one or more of the five senses. Any undergraduate trained in American poetry has heard the maxim "No ideas but in things," advice given by the master of the literal image, William Carlos Williams, author of one of the most famous Imagist poems: *so much depends / upon // a red wheel / barrow // glazed with rain / water // beside the white / chickens.* Though the image takes root in what we see, smell, touch, taste, and feel in this world, the five senses are, at the same time, as William Blake writes in *The Marriage of Heaven and Hell,* our "chief inlets of Soul in this age." [1] The literal or concrete image, as writers and readers know, has the paradoxical capacity to turn figurative, to transform from "thing" to not only "idea" but feeling, inspiration, even theophany.

What is an image? We speak of it as literal or figurative, concrete or surreal, fragmented or narrative, as symbol, referent, whether juxtaposed disjointedly or occurring serially. It has been defined simply as an object in the world, which the poet represents mimetically, and complexly, initiating philosophical discussions of the relation between subject and object. Simile, metaphor, personification, allegory, analogy, and symbol are forms of it. In modern and contemporary poetry, it has been the source of formal investigation for poets from H.D. to Williams to Oppen to Wright to Levertov. Imagism, "the *point de repère* usually and conveniently taken as the starting point of modern poetry," [2] T.S. Eliot claims, speaking of the particular Anglo-American and English movement that aimed at freeing the image from its previous symbolic and emotional baggage and, thus, allowing it to stand on its own. Ezra Pound, more intriguingly, called it "an intellectual and emotional complex in an instant of time."[3]

"An image," John Berger writes, in his book *Ways of Seeing,* "is a sight which has been recreated or reproduced. It is an appearance, or a set of appearances, which has been detached from the place and time in which it first made its appearance and preserved—for a few moments or a few centuries."[4] What I am specifically concerned with in this book is their "re-appearance," and subsequent "re-creation," in meditative and poetic practice, and how poetry facilitates and transforms the initial apperception of "a thing" into something more closely resembling a dialogue between object and subject. Most importantly, I am interested in the potential of the image—particularly the natural image, the image from the non-human world—to bridge the increasing rift between human consciousness and nature's consciousness, to investigate how "the shaping spirit of Imagination," as Samuel Taylor Coleridge called it, might help unite "the living self to the living outer world." [5]

What the chickadees bring to our encounter and what I bring have equal weight. This emotional and intellectual and visual and auditory complex or matrix or pattern of exchanges is at the root of what makes us human. Anthropological evidence suggests that the transformation from the Neanderthal brain to that of the *homo sapiens* made it possible to actually *see or imagine* oneself and, so, to compare oneself with other species, to remember the migratory routes and seasons of plants and animals, and to plan toward the future. It gave us an advantage. It has also given us language. Through the reading of words or hearing of words, we are able to picture things we haven't experienced ourselves. This image-making ability of the mind involves memory, but it is also creative. It enables us to locate and embody the invisible and the unknown.

Image: *luminous particular, epiphany, inscape, objective correlative, adequate symbol, apparition, apperception, spots of time, thing*—the "natural object" or image has assumed many names and been employed to explain the intricacies of various and often-conflicting philosophies and poetics. It has served many masters as a pivot around which the central tenets of romanticism, Imagism, modernism, surrealism, and postmodernism might be argued. Yet the thing itself, the natural image seen not as object but as being in living relationship to ourselves as other living beings on this planet, as subject with its own claims, is something poetry—and humanity— is still trying to accomplish. M.H. Abrams, writing in *Natural Supernaturalism* about the central place of nature in romantic poetics, says, "The illuminated phenomenal object, if transparent to a significance beyond itself, reappears as the symbol of the Symbolists, but if opaque, as the image of the Imagists; in both cases, however, the Romantic object is usually cut off from its context in the ordinary world and in common experience and assigned an isolated existence in the self-limited and self-sufficing work of art."[6] If one believes, as I do, that poetry teaches us how to live, not just how to write, in what ways can the image help to solve or salve or satisfy the conundrum of both seeing and being? In which ways can it teach us to turn to, not from, an earth we are perilously close to ruining for ourselves as well as for the non-human?

II

IN A STATION OF THE METRO

*The apparition of these faces in the crowd;*
*Petals on a wet, black bough.*

When Ezra Pound began writing "In a Station of the Metro," in 1912, he saw his task clearly as rendering his "intuition" or feeling of the images assailing him as he emerged from a train station in Paris. As he wrote about it later:

> I saw suddenly a beautiful face, and then another and another, and then a beautiful child's face, and then another beautiful woman, and I tried all that day to find words that seemed to me worthy, or as lovely as that sudden emotion. And that evening, as I went home along the Rue Raynourd, I was still trying, and I found, suddenly, the expression. I do not mean that

I found words, but there came an equation . . . not a speech, but in little splotches of color. It was just that—"a pattern," or hardly a pattern, if by "pattern" you mean something with a "repeat" in it. But it was a word, the beginning, for me, of a language in color . . .[7]

Pound was clearly uninterested in representing only the concrete, objective reality of the moment. Like other modernists, he rejected the idea of art as simply mimesis, or mirror of the outer world. What he was after was a poem that included his intuition of the beauty and brevity of the moment, an intuition that included *all he could not find words for,* something bigger than mere representation.

He had been translating the poems of the Chinese. In them, he had found a method that expressed, in as few words as possible, one image—precisely, clearly, perfectly—and set it on top of another which did the same. He called this method super-positioning. It took him a year to pare down his impressions into the two lines we have come to know this famous poem by. What makes his discovery so revolutionary is the way in which the two images—that of the crowd and that of the flowering branches in the rain—exist not as similes or metaphors, not as one image compared or qualified by the other, but as contingent. Whether the poet saw the flowers, the rain, or the faces in his mind or on the street does not matter. They came to him together; they appeared side by side. Their contingency—the contingency of images that exists in any moment intensely perceived—created a resonance between them, and, through the poem, a new method of apprehension.

Of course, the danger in this kind of image-making is the danger that led many of the original *Imagistes* to abandon poems which stood like statues in a museum of caught moments, of light or wind, of miniatures of weather. To render the image with concrete intensity and precision was also to freeze it in time and place. The red wheel barrow glazed with rain water, though awakening us to the beauty of momentary things, was not large enough to contain a response to the increasingly chaotic and violent world that Europeans, including American expatriates Pound, H.D., and Eliot, found themselves overwhelmed by. The solution to this, for many poets, was to accumulate many images, juxtaposed against each other, to gather patterns of images into open fields or larger stories of quests, searches, and journeys toward a meaning.

Pound collected and arranged disparate images in his book-length *Cantos* with the intention that, given enough of them, they would cohere into a larger explanation of the world, much as the German romantic poet Novalis tried to collect fragments for a *Romantic Encyclopaedia* or *Scientific Bible.*[8] Novalis and Pound, like Joyce in

*Ulysses,* H.D. in *Trilogy,* and Eliot in *The Waste Land,* believed in the possibility of a wholeness, perceivable and expressible, that if they could amass enough particulars, they, as creative beings, could see *into* a cohesiveness beyond the surface confusion. If they could create enough versions, they could create a vision. Pound ended the *Cantos* by famously saying, "I cannot make it cohere." [9] Novalis, who abandoned his project, wrote, "Only the fragment appears most bearable." [10] Eliot spoke of *The Waste Land* as "These fragments I have shored against my ruins." [11] H.D. wrote, in her prose memoir *Tribute to Freud,* "There are priceless broken fragments that are meaningless until we find the other broken bits to match them." [12]

That the image is a fragment of an original whole is a notion we find in Plato, in the Kabbalah, in Hermeticism and many other mystery religions, a notion based, according to M.H. Abrams in *Natural Supernaturalism*, on the premise that humanity began in unity and departs increasingly into division and conflict, that "the cosmic course is from the One and the Good into evil and multiplicity and back to the One." [13] The fragmentation and disjunction we experience in contemporary life, as well as in contemporary poetry, is not exactly new, though it is exacerbated by the fast pace and avalanche of information with which we are now assailed. Abrams writes that, in marked contrast to the viewpoints of many poets writing today, romantic and modernist poets still worked toward a "reconciliation and redemption" that might be achieved, if not through religion, at least through art. Even Pound did not give up his belief in the possibility of cohesion: "i.e. it coheres all right / even if my notes do not cohere," he writes. [14]

"The modern way of seeing is to see in fragments," writes Susan Sontag in one of her last essays, "A Little Summa," about the photographic image. "It is felt that reality is essentially unlimited, and knowledge is open-ended. It follows that all boundaries, all unifying ideas have to be misleading, demagogic; at best, provisional; almost always, in the long run, untrue." [15] The first surrealist movement, occurring as it did between the wars (the first *Surrealist Manifesto* was published in 1924), was a response to just this kind of demagogy, the idea that we can think our way through to wholeness, that if we gather enough information, garner enough facts, we can solve any problem, an idea obviously discredited in the aftermath of the First World War. Better to learn to live with contradiction, variety, disjunction, discontinuity, than to become comfortable with only one definition of reality, imposed by religion or politics or the marketplace, than to agree to fascism. Surrealism, with its emphasis on images drawn from dreams, the wildness of chance, and unconscious desire, extended our definition of the real by opening the conscious mind to realms of perception hitherto unknown or agreed upon. For André Breton, surrealism was not a replacement of the real with the unreal, but an enlargement, a *surreality* whose aim was nothing less than, Breton states in his *Second Manifesto,* "total recovery of our psychic force." [16]

The method of access to this force for poets was automatic writing, a technique coterminous with, as well as influenced by, Freud's psychoanalytic technique of "free association." The images that washed up on the shores of the surrealist poem were recognizably different, strange and incoherent: *The exquisite corpse shall drink the new wine. The wounded women disturb the guillotine with blond hair.* They flirted with madness, even meaninglessness. More importantly, collage—the surrealists' preferred method of assembling these fragments, whether in poetry or visual art—emphasized arbitrary and extreme juxtapositions, even collisions. Surrealism enacted a revolution in use of the image that crosses cultures and spans the years between its inception and contemporary poetry today. Offshoots of French surrealism include the Latin American surrealism of Pablo Neruda, a precursor of magic realism; the post-colonial surrealism of the Caribbean poets like Aimé Césaire; Lorca's dark Andalusian rendition of the Deep Song; the American Deep Image poets, influenced by Neruda, as well by Robert Bly's translations of Tranströmer and Rilke (what Andrew Joron calls the "allegorizing Eastern European mode of surrealism"),[17] and later, poets of the Beat era, collage poets, poets exploring the arrangement of images in non-narrative, disjunctive and, to borrow a word from the surrealists, *convulsive* ways, all influenced by the freedom to go beyond the boundaries of the concrete for images. The image, *as* fragment, or rather, as discontinuous accumulation of fragments, bound by chance encounters in dreams and waking life, gave us a glimpse into an entirely different way of envisioning our world.

The source of the surrealist image, however, is debatable. In Spanish surrealism, of which Federico Garcia Lorca is representative, the duende, not the unconscious, was the source. For Lorca, the duende was a power, which he described as "the sound of the dark": "These 'dark sounds' are the mystery, the roots thrusting into the fertile loam known to all of us, ignored by all of us, but from which we get what is real in art."[18] In his well-known essay "Theory and Function of the *Duende,*" he states that this mysterious power is "in fact the spirit of the earth."[19] Neruda, too, felt that the power of the image—although he always acknowledged his debt to the French surrealists—came not only from accessing the unconscious but from encountering other forms of life outside the human mind. In an interview with Robert Bly in 1966, he states,

I am not a theoretician, but I do see as one kind of poetry the poetry which is written in closed rooms. I'll give as an example Mallarmé, a very great French poet. I have sometimes seen photographs of his room; they were full of little beautiful objects—*abanicos*—fans. He used to write beautiful poems on fans. But his rooms are stuffy, all full of curtains, no air. He is a great poet of closed rooms and it seems that many of the New World poets follow this tradition: they don't open the windows and you not only have to open the window but come through the windows and live with rivers and animals and beasts.[20]

The tension between this suddenly accessible and at the same time irrational interior world of the unconscious and the so-called living exterior of "rivers and animals and beasts" can be seen in a wide and divergent range of subsequent poetries. There is the late French surrealism of René Char, for example, translated here by Mary Ann Caws:

> *Born of the call of becoming and the anguish of retention, the poem, rising from its well of mud and stars, will bear witness, almost silently, that there was nothing in it that did not truly exist elsewhere, in this rebellious and solitary world of contradictions.*[21]

Char's images are often contradictory—"Moderate as stone, I remain a mother with far away candles"—and ambiguous, in keeping with the surrealist project to break from the inherent restrictions of grammar and logic. Unlike the earlier surrealists, Char's poetry, especially after the Second World War, when he was a leader in the French Resistance, took its images, from both inner and outer worlds, from the violence of war and the beauty of his rural village of Vaucluse and from his intensely hermetic and dreamlike inner world. In speaking of an officer from North Africa who is, he says, " hardened against [the partisans'] 'images in speech,'" he reminds him that this kind of language "comes from the sense of wonder communicated by the beings and things we live with in continual intimacy."[22]

In reading Char, who seems to utilize the image to render the phenomenal world and its mysterious undercurrent at the same time—as Helen Vendler says, "he writes with absolute candor, but in a secret language"[23]—I realize the difficulty of coming to any strict definition of the image. It is, rather, the *experience* of the image that the image makes possible. As the Syrian poet Adonis, influenced both by Sufism and European surrealism, writes, the image is "a penetrating, revealing light directed at the unknown. The image is a becoming, a change of state." [24] The attempt at forging a union of opposites, Adonis says, is "the supreme point" in Breton's *Second Manifesto,* the reaching of which was surrealism's ultimate motive. The Sufis, he says, describe this point as "the place in which the inner being, the essence and the outer being, the subject meet."[25] At this point, contradictions vanish.

It can safely be said that all manner of images are concurrent in contemporary poetry. One can find concrete images, figurative images, fragmented images, surrealist images, disjunctive and recurring images, images arranged in narrative or collage, symbols, allegories, analogies, metaphors, similes . . . even an absence or ellipsis of them, all of them even within one poem or series of poems. And, although the range of image-making practices is wide, for all their substantive differences— whether we are speaking of romantic epics, Imagist lyrics, modernist collections of the fragment, or surrealist collage—they return us to certain questions: How can the image lead us past that ultimate contradiction, the relation of the fragment to the whole? For even the gathering of fragments into larger narratives, whether cohesive or disjunctive, must be, in the end, fragmentary. Seeing in parts is a condition of our time, or rather, *of time.* That the whole slips away from us is related to our transience, to the way all is here for a short interval and then gone, including our lives. Yet the power of the exterior image does resonate in us, and the interior image, if expressed, will often open to a vista and vision beyond us, bringing us back, with new eyes, to the mystery of the concrete world.


But what about life out there, alone by itself, that small boat? What about all the deer feeding without us in the moonlight, the river, which has risen and quickened, brown now with the all-day rain, the "speaking face of earth and heaven," as Wordsworth called it, not as objective correlative, not willed, not word, but here, encountered, influencing us? *Influence,* meaning influential, a flowing in. *The supposed flowing of an ethereal fluid or power from the stars. The effect of an external field.* The image, like music, is a common language. It is the language of the external field. Conversely, or inversely, it is also the language of the interior life, of dreams, visions, some would even say thoughts.

This book consists of eight essays on the life of the image, and its role in visionary experience, through a range of cultural practices, focusing primarily on poetry but including painting, sculpture, and song. It is not meant to be a mapping, however abbreviated or incomplete, of the various appearances of the image in the history of poetry, though it does engage with this history, as well as with contemporary poets, philosophers, archeologists, artists, and cultural critics whose work explores the image and how it might help us to navigate the almost impossibly large subject of the human in relation to the natural world. Instead, in investigating the differences between image and vision, allegory and symbol, the abstract and the concrete, my intention is to explore the question: how might we draw on our encounters, whether we are writers or not, to enlarge our consciousness as human beings, and thus, to live more wholly?

Plants, birds, flowers, branches, wind, even the dead—each essay examines the dual life of the image as both earthly and symbolic presence and investigates ways that poets, especially, but also painters, sculptors, and other seers have encountered it as a way to traverse the boundaries between the self and these other presences. Beginning, in the first essay, "Learning to Speak with Them," with a discussion of traditional American Indian songs, the essays focus on specific forms of the literary image, whether symbolic, metaphoric, literal, or allegorical, and range widely in subject, from pre-contact Ojibwa chants to a 12th century Persian epic, from modernist poems by Pound, H.D., and Rilke, to work by contemporary poets such as Mei Mei Berssenbrugge, Christopher Howell, Kamau Brathwaite, Brenda Hillman, Lucille Clifton, and Ko Un. Three of the essays focus on the work of visual artists. "The Imaginal Book of Cave Paintings" is a study of the pictographs and petroglyphs scattered on the bluffs, cave walls, cliffs, and rock shelters in Montana and the West as "a visionary record, a record of the visionary that spans thousands of years, perhaps thousands of people." Rock art, painted and etched by people anywhere from 18,000 to 500 years ago, is compelling, not only in the knowledge it provides about the ceremonial relationship of early peoples to the earth, but also in our own imaginative relation to it. Drawing on poets such as Clayton Eschleman and Adonis, and writers as diverse as John Berger, Robert Pogue Harrison, Henry Corbin, Gaston Bachelard, Maurice Merleau-Ponty, and Mircea Eliade, as well as numerous archeologists, these essays investigate the pictorial image as an imaginary art of the interior.

How do we "talk with the image"? How do we stand in the threshold between our outer and inner perceptions of it, closer to the language of the mixed flock of chickadee and nuthatch, both red breasted and white, the two Clark's nutcrackers, and the one stellar jay who appear at my feeder and in my dreams? How do we live as people of the Image, "rising from its well of mud and stars," in relation to it? What are the techniques we would need? "The triumph of public reason," writes

Tom Cheetham, "is evident in the modern world. The absence of the fragile world of interiority, of vessels that contain the water of life, the inability of so many people to find, or even know how to seek any 'innerness'—all this is driving us crazy." [26] To shore up the crossbeams of the interior world in order for it to be ready to welcome what is outside it, one must be willing to allow the world to speak, willing to listen for correspondences between human consciousness and the consciousnesses of the natural world. To open ourselves to this news requires a poet's attentiveness, something we might learn from poetry. "All of us," Cheetham writes, "however dimly, perceive events in the imaginal world, and the task of transformation requires the development of the senses that open us into that world." [27] All that is unknown is invisible. Is not an image. And yet is incipient in it.

LEARNING TO SPEAK WITH THEM

Suppose you are walking in a place you have frequented enough to be stopped by the deep-shaded green the spruce has turned in summer. Perhaps you even notice how it grows singular, unattended, unlike the Douglas fir and lodge pole pine that crowd the slopes above it, how it lives where it can soak its roots in the creek. You might even know this tree's name—Engelmann—and that it needs this unshared light around it. You stop. It is so beautiful. You want to draw it toward you. You'd like to know something of what it knows. Perhaps it could teach you how to live.

Should you kneel below it? Should you touch it, gaze up through its branches? And does it really matter how you approach it? Basho records how the peasants dressed in their finest to climb the mountain passes. The Cree here in Montana smudge themselves with smoking sweetgrass or cedar before they gather herbs or cut down an aspen. How to speak to it? Well, easy it is to speak. But you're not looking for ordinary speech as commerce, as Stephané Mallarmé writes, speech as "a commercial approach to reality."[1] You want something deeper, a communication, a communion.

One place to find a tradition of communicating with plants and animals, with the non-human (a phrase I will use instead of the word "nature"), is in the oral poetry and transcribed songs of the Native American tribes:

> How shall I begin my songs
> In the blue night that is settling?
>
> In the great night my heart will go out,
> Toward me the darkness comes rattling.
> In the great night my heart will go out.[2]

In a traditional song such as this Papago "Owl Woman Song," what is immediately striking to me is the indeterminate nature of speaker and addressee. Who is speaking to whom? The speaker could be at once owl (personification), human becoming owl (metaphor), or human addressing owl (apostrophe), going out to meet its "darkness" halfway. Owl/woman: the poem enacts both realities at once—one speaks to the owl, yet, at the same time, one is speaking for it. Or rather, in order to speak for the owl, one must speak as it; the speaker, thus, is both transcriber of song and creator of song, both listener and singer.

SONG OF THE THUNDERS

Sometimes I
Go about pitying
Myself
While I am carried by the wind
Across the sky.[3]

Though transcribed from their native languages by the ethnomusicologist Frances Densmore only two or three generations ago, these songs, given to the singer through the spirit of the plant or animal, seem ancient. They seem to belong not only to another people but to another world, a world that was not, we are taught, real. "Before I came on this world," said the Crow medicine woman Pretty Shield to Frank B. Linderman in 1932, "and even for a time afterward, my people saw strange things, heard words spoken that they did not always understand. Now, they see nothing, hear nothing that is strange."[4]

This *strangeness*, this sense of being able to transverse worlds, is an aim we see again and again in poem-making. The desire to disperse or de-center the self, evidenced in many contemporary texts, is part of a larger tradition that can be traced back to poetry's origins in prayer, prophesy, and spell. What poets are importantly interested in: when another voice takes over. What we name that voice—the muse of the Greeks, the Imagination of the romantics, the unconscious of the surrealists, the duende of Andalusian flamenco singers—of course, has fluctuated. And yet, as André Breton writes, "we still know as little as we ever did about the origin of the voice which it is everyone's prerogative to hear, if only he will, a *voice* which converses with us most specifically about something other than what we believe we are thinking."[5]

When we use the word *voice* in regard to poetry, we usually mean the voice the poet speaks with, though that voice can be dispersed across different figures within the text. Voice usually includes choices in diction, syntax, rhythm, and image. Yet how does the world speak to us? What voices do we hear, as opposed to speak with? And how is a translation made? What I have learned from the traditional Native people here in Montana is that the songs one sings in the ceremonies are owned by the singer. One can ask for someone else's song, but only by going through the proper rituals. One can never buy a song. Initially, a song must be given by the spirit of the being one contacts, whether that being is the eagle, the aspen, the sky or the earth, such as in this description of a young man's vision quest by the Sioux spiritual leader Black Elk: "He must be careful less distracting thoughts come to him, yet he must be alert to recognizing any messenger which the Great Spirit may send him for these people often come in the form of an animal, even one as small and as seemingly insignificant as the little ant." [6] Through fasting, prayer and ritual purification, the seeker was able to commune with the non-human and transform that communion into language, into an art form he or she could use. Once a song is made, it unites both singer and spirit. If one continues to sing and then neglects the source of that song, at best the spirit will leave the singer; at worst it could drive her mad. In other words, the making of a song proposes a path, a relationship.

❅

OREAD

Whirl up, sea,
whirl your pointed pines,
splash your great pines
on our rocks,
hurl your green over us,
cover us with your pools of fir. [7]

In his working papers, the poet George Oppen writes that he could never have written a poem such as H.D.'s "Oread"; he could never think to command the sea. [8] Whether it is the sea that is addressed or the sea of trees that make up the forest covering the mountains in Pennsylvania, where H.D. grew up, a wooded slope incipient with wind, is disputable. An oread is a mountain spirit. Is the poet then adopting the persona of the spirit of the mountain commanding its forces? Or is the speaker a woman conjuring—rather than commanding—the mountain spirit, in this case its manifestation as wind? The poem has the purposefulness of a spell, of something set in motion by the act of its being spoken. Conjure: *to summon in a sacred name, to enjoin.* As in the Native American examples before it, there is, in "Oread," an indeterminacy of speaker and addressee, a voice shift flickering back and forth between the you and I. One might call it multiple subjectivity. One might also call it what Sufi scholar Henri Corbin names, in his discussion of the creative imagination, "a dialogical situation." [9]

It would be helpful here to look at the term "creative imagination" and to try to separate it from the diminished meaning with which we have come to regard the imaginary—as fantasy, unreality, un-tethered association, a simile-making machine. Ralph Waldo Emerson uses the term "active imagination" in his essay "The Poet," and defines it as "a very high sort of seeing, which does not come by study, but by the intellect being where and what it sees; by sharing the path or circuit of things through forms, and so making them translucid to others." [10] H.D.'s method speaks of a similar translation through forms. "We begin with sympathy of thought," she writes in *Notes on Thought and Vision*, a book-length essay in which she explains her method of generating images as an action described in the figure of a jelly fish: "When the center of consciousness and the jelly-fish is in the body (I visualize it in my case lying on the left side with streamers or feelers floating up toward the brain) we have vision of the womb or love-vision." [11] The imagination, in this case, is conceived as an act rather than a quality or description (as in *imaginary*), as a movement out from the body and toward its subject, whether the thought of the subject or the existence of the subject itself.

H.D. uses the precision she learned in her early Imagist practice to describe the wind in trees for us. At the same time, she conjures a mythological or hermetic being, a figure "entering the imagination," according to Adelaide Morris, "from another dimension and carrying with [it] the mysterious radiance by which H.D. gratefully remapped our 'dead, old, thousand times explored old world.'" [12] Yet the subject of H.D.'s poem is not only the oread, I would argue, despite its Greek title. Could the poem not at the same time be read as adopting a voice which co-exists with us here on earth and yet is other—the wind, the trees, the wind-in-the-trees?

This dual life—the image as both earthly presence and symbolic presence, both literal and figurative—is something one recognizes in the Native American examples. At the same time that there is a particular owl being addressed, there is the sense of owl as representation or earthly manifestation of Owl People. How then do these exist at the same time and how are both existences quickened when the poem or song is spoken or sung? In his book *Creative Imagination in the Sufism of Ibn Arabi*, Corbin uses the term "creative imagination" or theophanic prayer to describe a technique employed by the Sufi mystics in ancient Iran. [13] It is a practice the Sufis used to visualize, and thus meet, the god-head, a method perhaps akin to H.D.'s. The practice depended on the positing of a three-fold vision of the world:

The World of Mystery

The World of Pure Images

The World of Our Senses

Between the World of Mystery, to which we have no direct access, and the concrete world perceivable by our five senses, is what Corbin calls the *"mundus imaginalis,"* an imaginal realm.[14] The creative imagination, he states, functions as an "intermediary, a mediatrix," [15] between these worlds. It shares, to repeat what Emerson says, "a path or circuit of things through forms." That circuit is the flicker between symbolic and concrete we often feel in any precisely rendered image. How to explain it? "The unity of being conditions the dialogical situation," Corbin writes. The Sufis did not "make things up" out of thin air. Their visions came in the forms of earthly things, in flowers, rivers, fountains, birds, animals, light.

If I substitute the word "being" or "life" for "The World of Mystery," I can find a way of thinking about the image and its use, at least in poetry, as a means of communication with the non-human. In many ways, our distrust of the symbol is a question of hermeneutics, of who or what gets to interpret the image. This is why the work of Corbin is instructive. The Sufis brought a hermeneutics of the heart to clerical Islam. They believed in their visions not because the visions reaffirmed an ecclesiastical interpretation but because they had created them; they had brought them into being in a form they could see and understand. Corbin says that the mystics, as differentiated from those who practiced the official religion of Islam, were after an individual, epiphanic experience. The goal of the "visionary recitals" (a practice so complex, hermetic, and committed that I do not pretend to understand it) was to meet with one's own personal manifestation of the divine. The power to create was granted by one's belief in the possibility of communion, a highly individualized communion in which the mystic and the god take part, a two-fold meeting for which both sides are responsible.

The question, though, for me remains: Is the rendering of precise image a form of attention to this world or a means of departure from it? Is the non-human another dimension we have been excluding or is the non-human a symbol masking a mystical or symbolic dimension, an other than earthly dimension? Do animals and plants stand for something else, and thus, lose their value as *beings that exist?* Are they not things in themselves, rich with knowledge of what it means to live on this earth, knowledge that is not ours?

❋

### THE SEA ROSE

Rose, harsh rose,
marred and with stint of petals,
meager flower, thin,
sparse of leaf,
more precious
than a wet rose
single on a stem—
you are caught in the drift. [16]

It is obvious that the sea rose in the above poem is a concrete, individual rose, that H.D. has seen it, is perhaps seeing it as she writes, that she is perhaps writing *en plein-air* as painters do. The image is precise and lean, a perfect example of an early Imagist poem, which Pound defined as "austere, direct, free from emotional slither." [17] But, though one of the aims of Imagism was to avoid solipsism, to let the image speak for itself without imposing meaning from without (cultural, historical, religious) and from within (the unconscious), H.D. also knew her Greek mythology, was conversant in hermetic lore; she was, as well, a student of Freud's. In this poem, the rose, a figure fraught with symbolic meaning, is described concretely. Yet because the poem is countering the traditional symbol of rose—this rose is harsh, not lovely; marred, not perfect; stinted, not voluptuous; beleaguered in the wild, not safe in a bouquet—it, too, begins to reflect a symbolic reality, even a subversive one. One does not think of a rose as "marred," "meager," "sparse." She tells us it is more precious. Why? Is it because it survives past our stereotypes of rose? Is it because it survives at all? And who, again, is speaking? The rose is addressed as a you. Is H.D. employing personification? Or is the poet "like" a rose, feeling stunted and flung about by the forces of the world? Or is she both, enacting the "dialogical situation" Corbin speaks of, the voice as both rose and poet?

Like H.D.'s early work in *Sea Garden*, Louise Glück's lyrically beautiful sequence of poems, *The Wild Iris*, takes as its point of attention various plants and flowers, specifically those growing in Glück's summer and end-of-summer garden: wild iris, trillium, poppies, clover, violets. The book begins with the title poem:

At the end of my suffering
there was a door.

Hear me out: that which you call death
I remember.

Overhead, noises, branches of the pine shifting.
Then nothing. The weak sun
flickered over the dry surface.[18]

At first glance, we assume that the iris is speaking; we might even sense the voice as a kind of conceit, a personification or instance of anthropomorphism, the iris as mask for the speaker. There is an "I" who is attempting to describe what happens when we die and what it might mean to live again. There is a "you" to whom this lesson is taught. The "you" has a word for the end of life—"death"—and so must be human. Yet as in the previous poems, the speaker—and the poems almost always use first person point of view—is indeterminate, often mysteriously. Does an iris "suffer?" And if the iris has died back at the end of its season, who then is describing "the weak sun?" It must be someone still here, someone who has also the word "door," who can still hear overhead the shifting of birds. It is as if the point of view had changed from plant to observer of plant, as if the speaker is both inside the experience and outside it, is a flower who suffers and one who can recognize an end to suffering, as if, as the poet Clayton Eshleman writes in *Juniper Fuse*, his mediation on the origin of images, "*seeing into* and *seeing through* combined into a winding window." [19]

The vegetative world gives literal evidence of the cycle of death and regeneration. An iris bulb, especially, which propagates by bulb and is perennial, will return each spring to the spot it has died back to. Flowers, for this reason, have heavy truck in our tradition as religious symbols of rebirth and redemption after suffering, of the spirit's winter and spring, night and dawn. The poem ends, "whatever / returns from oblivion returns / to find a voice: / from the center of my life came / a great fountain, deep blue / shadows on azure seawater." Flowers are the most silent of things. Their voice comes to us in shape and color. Glück identifies the speaker not as iris, but as consciousness. But whose? Identity flickers as the sun does on the dry ground from flower to human to a widely dispersed god as gardener, or gardener as god. The image of a fountain might refer to the god of the Old Testament. Or it could be Orpheus who suffered the grief of love, descended to the underworld and came up singing. Or it could be Jesus who blossomed out of his cave.

When Ezra Pound states in his Imagist manifesto that "the natural object is always the *adequate* symbol," one could read the statement as an attempt to grant the world its autonomy, in effect, to grant the non-human world its voice. Pound uses the term phanopoeia to describe "the casting of images upon the visual imagination of the reader, crediting the early Chinese poets as being adept at this. "In phanopoeia," he writes, "we find the greatest drive toward precision of the word." [20] However, Glück's flowers are not only precisely described; they speak. They speak not only of the biological life cycle of a flower but of redemption, atonement, resurrection, belief and disbelief, all notions deeply connotative of a Judeo-Christian tradition. Seven poems are entitled "Matins" and ten "Vespers." Many address a god in Western patriarchal terms: "Unreachable father." The natural object as adequate symbol? The phrase seems a paradoxical one. Is it possible to see the thing itself?

The confusion, it seems to me, can be located in the nature of the symbol itself. When Charles Baudelaire writes, in his famous poem "Correspondences," that "man passes through forests of symbols / Which observe him with familiar eyes," [21] he is speaking to the "doctrine of correspondences," a doctrine posited by eighteenth century mystic Emanuel Swedenborg who believed, like the Sufi mystics Corbin studied, that the sensory world is a reflection of a parallel corresponding world of spirit. In fact, one of the tenets of French symbolism—whose adherents were familiar with the writings of Swedenborg—was a profound belief that the world speaks to us. I have often wondered if the *haunting objects* [22] that permeated the imaginations of the romantics and symbolists—the rose, the swan, the albatross— are so very different in function from the haunting objects of the tribal people in America—the eagle, the bear, the water panther. Yet there are profound differences. Because, before symbolism—and I am speaking here of the symbolism for which Mallarmé was spokesman—the nature of an object was assigned to a meaning bound to one's time and culture, however circumscribed or open-ended, whether tribal, Christian, Hindu, Eastern, Western. Each symbol is created, maintained, and interpreted in light of generations of stories and songs that come down through cultural history. To let go the rein of traditional hermeneutics was one of the aims of the symbolist movement, to free the image so it could be free-floating, un-interpreted, and thus, remain numinous, maintaining its own life as object. Mallarmé recognized the power in certain images and yet, he felt that to explain or describe them robs them of their mystery: "It is not description which can unveil the efficacy and beauty of monuments, seas, or the human face in all their maturity and native state, but rather evocation, *allusion, suggestion*." [23] His ideal poem would allow the concrete object to suggest its symbolic reality, if only for us to feel, never interpret, the life-force behind it.

According to *The New Princeton Encyclopedia of Poetry and Poetics*, Mallarmé believed that "the creation of the symbol occurs in two ways: a haunting object permeates little by little the consciousness of the poet and is associated with a state of being of which the poet was not initially aware. The other direction of the image/mood association is from the inside outward: a state of being or an unnamable feeling is projected onto an exterior world, targeting an object or landscape which gives it embodiment." [24] What is key here is that the symbol is "created." It is made by the intersection of the concrete object and the gazing subject; in terms of this essay, between the non-human and the poet. What is the nature of that intersection? Mallarmé does not differentiate between the two methods of creating the symbol, whether from attention to something that calls to the poet or whether from the poet departing from herself toward her object. According to Corbin, it is the same for the Sufi mystics: "To say that one of our thoughts, sentiments, or desires is concretized in a form specific to the intermediate plane of Idea-Images of subtle matter is the same as to meditate before a flower, a mountain or a constellation in order to discover not what obscure and unconscious force they manifest, but what divine thought, flowering in the world of spirit, is epiphanized, is at work in them."[25]

Mallarmé was only mildly interested in the concrete object, the real swan or deer in the forest. The object existed only as doorway to symbolic encounter, and, once passed through, lost its necessity and, quite properly, should disappear: "Why should we perform the miracle by which a natural object is almost made to disappear beneath the magic waving wand of the written word, if not to divorce that object from the direct and the palpable, and so conjure up its *essence* in all purity." [26] Can we have both the direct and palpable, which Mallarmé denounces, along with "the forest's shuddering," which he advocates for? Can we respect both the concrete and symbolic reality of the forms of life before us? Can poetry do this, enact what is essentially a transference, a communion with another without weighing the encounter down with outworn systems, leaving the interpretation of the image up for grabs, or vacating the object altogether? The danger of a poetics of attention is that we will project our desires onto the object, that in our departure we return to the self or culture we were trying to escape.

※

> In the small beauty of the forest
> The wild deer bedding down—
> That they are there! [27]

In George Oppen's well-known poem "Psalm," the first stanza asserts the right of the deer to exist in themselves and not as symbols. The poet sees and praises the fact of the deer's presence with Imagist precision, detailing the roots which "dangle from their mouths / scattering earth in the strange woods" and how "their alien small teeth / tear at the grass." How astonishing, the poet seems to be saying. "They who are there," he repeats, who are there and astonishingly not us. Oppen seems intent on seeing only what *is*, to find words, simple words arranged in a way that would "construct meaning" that would awaken us to the reality of our existence on earth. "If we were born, full blown, in space," he writes in one of his daybooks, "a planet hanging enormously in front of us, no one would hunt for misty words or for 'mysticism.' One would say look! Or, do you see it? Or What is it? I should suppose that nothing—nothing at all—but the constant repetition of abstract words could blind us to that presence." [28] The poem ends:

> The small nouns
> Crying faith
> In this in which the wild deer
> Startle, and stare out.

There are many ways to read this poem—and many contemporary schools of poetics have claimed Oppen for their own. Most would agree that part of his project is to render experience objectively, to attend to it without symbol or decoration, to attend without self-regard or self-mystification. Oppen's "Psalm" makes no large claims; it is a "small" beauty that is going to be described. He will use "small" nouns in order to do this. He will try to get out of the way.

Any naming is evidence of a desire for an encounter, of a "faith" that words will draw us closer. Unlike H.D., Oppen would never presume to speak for the deer. He does, however, speak to the distance that divides them. After all, are the woods "strange" to Oppen or to the deer? Are their teeth "alien" to him or to the grass? Do the words he uses to describe this experience—his own experience of it— separate him or bring him closer? Oppen is astonished that the deer are there, yet implicit in his statement is the fact that he is also astonished that we are. Because of the acute attention Oppen pays not only to the deer but to his experience of *meeting* the deer, there is, as in the many poems cited, a moment where we can feel that meeting as it might feel from both sides: hesitant, quiet, careful, startled. The deer stares out of its particular world as Oppen stares out of his. One is startled that another world exists beyond the self. This startling is a perception of difference that both deer and person share. How does the poem manage this transference? With respect, Oppen might answer, as he does in another poem, "The Hills," with respect and a conviction to honor the other in its other life, to attend, to be present in that meeting:

> That this is I,
> Not mine, which wakes
> To where the present
> Sun pours in the present, to the air perhaps
> Of love and of
> Conviction.[29]

Much contemporary poetry, as well as the means used to construct it— occlusion, omission, elision—avoids interpreting the image or connecting strings of images, letting, as Mallarmé would say, the silences speak. What might be found in those silences? One of the reasons I have been stressing the image when, paradoxically, I am writing about communication, is because obviously we do not share a language with non-human forms of life. "The paths of things are silent," Emerson writes. "Will they suffer a speaker to go with them? A spy they will not suffer; a lover, a poet, is the transcendency of their own nature." [30] In a world that seems increasingly focused on the needs of humans, when plants and animals are dying out at an alarming rate, the struggle to widen the world to one where we exist *in relation to* other forms of life seems crucial. Examining the ways poets both "read" and render that relation might help us effect a transcendence of our own.

L ess than an hour's drive north of Baghdad, near the Tigris River at Camp Anaconda: whiskered terns, white-cheeked bulbuls, white-breasted kingfishers, a squacco heron, purple swamp hen, spectacular hoopoe. The American soldier Jonathan Trouern-Trend, who counted them, says, in his book *Birding Babylon: A Soldier's Journal from Iraq*, "something as universally familiar as the migration of birds, or watching ducks in a pond, fulfilled a need to know that something worthwhile or even magical was happening, even in the midst of suicide bombings and rocket attacks." [1]

What kind of people "bird" or are "birders"? For those who love birds, each sighting, each recognition, is like a still life moving. Each bird is a stained glass window in a cathedral of place, telling the story not of a god slain but of song, costume, and the open road. I sometimes think of these sightings as reliquaries or a *retablo*, an overhanging altar for lights and ornaments, something filled with emblematic moments, as Joseph Cornell filled his boxes with coins, shells, and feathers—and Cornell made many boxes with birds or bird themes. In an interview with John Seabrook, Trouern-Trend asserts that, to be civilized, one should recognize the song and the sight of birds where one lives, much as one learns the area's history, its famous names and houses and events. [2] To know marks one's spot on the map, pins one's attention to the plants and animals within the varying circumference of what we call place and time. For birds, who migrate, who often breed and feed in quite different lands, place is, rather, the memory of a trajectory.

Why birds travel thousands of miles twice a year, traversing the earth in a star-navigated, blood-roused, or genetically programmed pilgrimage is one of our largest mysteries, and, of course, prime for allegory. The Latin word for birds, *aves*, originally meant both bird and spirit. It also meant "Hail," as well as

"Farewell." Allegories of the spirit ascending—as eagle for shamans, as hawk for the Egyptians—or descending—as dove or angels with their two, three, and four wings—are familiar to us. Daedalus invented wings so he and his son Icarus could escape the Labyrinth. Those who fly the highest are usually accorded the status of those closest to god. The ability to turn into a bird was common to all forms of shamanism. Flight, thus, is an image of freedom for those of us who are earthbound and longing for transcendence or transformation beyond the bounds of the self.

> Salutation, O Pigeon. Intone your notes so that I may scatter round you seven plates of pearls. Since the collar of faith encircles your neck it would not become you to be unfaithful.[3]

In the Persian epic poem, *The Conference of the Birds*, written by Farid ud-Din Attar in the twelfth century in northern Iran, twenty-two species of birds assemble and enact, in their migration, the allegory of a spiritual quest. The poem begins with an evocation by the poet, who greets the birds individually and reminds them that their mission is to seek god, who takes the form, in this text, of a king named Simorgh. It is a difficult enterprise; the group must traverse seven valleys: the Valley of the Quest, of Love, of Insight into Mystery, of Detachment, of Unity, of Bewilderment, and lastly, the Valley of Poverty and Nothingness.[4] That there will be trials at each stage of the journey is something we expect from this kind of quest, that there will be successes and failures. There is no guarantee that any of them will make it, and most of them won't. Indeed, at the end, only thirty do.

> Salutations, O gently moaning Turtle Dove! You went out contented and returned with a sad heart to a prison as narrow as Jonah's. O you who wander here and there like a fish, can you languish in ill-will? Cut off the head of this fish so that you may preen yourself on the summit of the moon.[5]

In *The Conference*, each bird comes to the quest with different attributes, different strengths and limitations. The poet welcomes, among others, the finch, parrot, partridge, falcon, magpie, heron, duck, goose, raven, hoopoe, dove, hawk, and peacock. The birds are soon aware that they are likely doomed—somewhat like characters in a novel by Beckett—and one by one they try to beg off, giving excuses for not participating. Their excuses are recognizable as *human* failings: the

Sparrow is too feeble and tender; the Peacock is vain and feels he is needed here; the Nightingale is too in love with the rose to leave. "O my friends," says the Partridge, "see how I live! Is it possible to awaken one who sleeps on stones and swallows gravel?" [6] The Owl says, "I have chosen for my dwelling a ruined and tumbledown house" and pleads, "I was born among the ruins and there I take my delight." [7] The Heron says, "I am so inoffensive that no one complains of me." [8]

Anthropomorphism, as a literary device, can be defined as the attributing of human characteristics to something not human. As a way of thought, it is impossible for us to avoid, given that being human is all we know. Personification, on the other hand, though it has come to mean the same thing, was originally, according to *The New Princeton Encyclopedia of Poetry and Poetics*, "the staging of personalities whose masks reveal" ideas or qualities. [9] For instance, Envy would take the stage, as would Avarice. A personification, thus, was a mask, a metaphor, a literal *figure of speech*. Personification, metaphor, and allegory have in common that they depend on an "undersense," and thus, consequently, an "oversense," the division of reality into both a concrete, sensory form and its underlying spiritual or ideational counterpart. Allegory correlates "different figures of a narrative with different levels of an orderly universe." [10] To work, of course, this kind of figure of speech depends on our belief that there *is* an underlying order.

In *The Conference of the Birds*, the birds don masks that can be attributed to various aspects of human personality. At the same time, it is also true that many of their qualities are ones we have perceived by living among them. It is not just ourselves but the sparrowness of the sparrow we recognize *in ourselves*, who builds homes and rarely strays from them, is industrious and devoted to its tribe; it is the resourcefulness, courage, and humor of the raven in the face of death, the patience of the pine siskin who waits all year for the pine seeds it is named for, the speed of hummingbirds who grab what they can when it's ripe. Could it be, not that the birds stand for our qualities, but rather that we, after observing them for generations, have learned how to be human *from* them?

Bruno Snell, in his book *The Discovery of Mind in Greek Philosophy and Literature*, elucidates this inverted, or rather, inflected way of looking at allegory. I quote at length:

> If the rock contributes to the understanding of a human attitude, i.e. if a dead object elucidates animate behavior, the reason is that the inanimate object is itself viewed anthropomorphically; the immobility of the boulder in the surf is interpreted as endurance, as a human being

endures in the midst of a threatening situation. It appears, therefore, that one object is capable of casting fresh light upon another in the form of a simile, only because we read into the object the very qualities which it in turn illustrates. . . . Thus it is not quite correct to say that the rock is viewed anthropomorphically, unless we add that our understanding of the rock is anthropomorphic for the same reason that we are able to look at ourselves petromorphically, and that the act of regarding the rock in human terms furnishes us with a means of apprehending and defining our own behavior. In other words, and this is all-important in any explanation of the simile, man must listen to an echo of himself before he may hear or know himself. [11]

Allegory is defined as a "term that denotes two complementary procedures: a way of composing literature and a way of interpreting it."[12] To compose allegorically is to construct a work so that its apparent sense refers to an "other" sense [i.e. each bird stands for a different kind of human attribute]. To interpret allegorically is to explain a work—or a world—as if there were an "other" sense to which it corresponds. The lives of birds are both compositional and interpretive. Each species of bird is tied genetically as well as through experience to changes in wind, light, and temperature. In turn, one could say that the literal and figurative nature of migration is the same. Migration is designed to ensure the survival not just of one bird, one self, but the whole of one's species, perhaps even the survival of all species. And, in fact, the thirty birds in *The Conference* who survive to make it to King Simorgh's residence find that what they have been searching for is this wholeness. According to the introduction in the Penguin translation of the epic, "The moment depends on a pun—only thirty *(si)* birds *(morgh)* are left at the end of the Way, and the *si morgh* meet the Simorgh, the goal of their quest." [13]

Welcome, O Hoopoe! You who were a guide to King Solomon and the true messenger of the valley, who had the good fortune to go to the borders of the Kingdom of Sheba.[14]

In the initial assembling of the birds in the Attar text, it is the hoopoe that is greeted first and who, subsequently, is voted in as the leader of the pilgrimage. I have never seen a hoopoe, yet most readers of Western literature have heard of it. In the famous story of Philomela, told in Ovid's *Metamorphosis*, it is the bird the rapist Tereus turns into after learning that his victim and her sister have fed him his son in revenge. They have transformed into a nightingale and a swallow in order to flee him:

One flew to the woods, the other to the roof-top,
And even so the red marks of the murder
Stayed on their breasts, the feathers were blood-colored.
Tereus, swift in grief and lust for vengeance,
Himself becomes a bird: a stiff crest rises
Upon the head, and a huge beak juts forward,
Not too unlike a sword. He is the hoopoe,
The bird who looks like war.[15]

The hoopoe often appears in Trauern-Trend's observations of Iraqi bird-life. Camp Anaconda is midpoint on the migration route for "species that breed in Europe and western Russia, and winter in Africa or the Middle East,"[16] and the hoopoe is just one of them. The birds, which frequent the dump and where the water drains from the laundry facility, seem un-phased by the war or destruction of land around them. For Trauern-Trend and many of his fellow soldiers, that fact was a solace, as birds have been, perhaps in any war. Philip Gosse, a medical officer in World War I, says, in Kenneth Helphand's book *Defiant Gardens: Making Gardens in Wartime*, that without the birds that shared the trenches he didn't think they could have gotten through at all. At a time when the no man's zone had become a virtual wasteland of stricken forests and scorched earth, that there were still birds helped to "stave off the men's despair at the horrors of the war."[17]

No one knows what the casualties of war amount to for the birds. Their needs are simple: water, a habitat that supports plant life for food, and shelter. Those are also our needs. Consequently, destroying habitat has always been a strategy of war. The Romans used to "salt the fields" around Carthage to impair food production. Jessica Adley and Andrea Grant report that, in South Vietnam, 14% of the forests were destroyed when the United States sprayed Agent Orange. "Few if any, have recovered. . . ."[18] There was the burning of 600 oil wells in the first Gulf War, which some environmentalists claim is the worst environmental disaster the world has yet suffered. Burning for nine months, they have changed the land and air irreparably. Then, there is the U.S. use of depleted uranium weapons, made from low-level radioactive waste, which we already know has caused mutations in human embryos along the line of those found in the vicinity of Chernobyl. Iraq's wetlands, like those in any arid place, are delicate. In fact, according to Solana Pyne, the huge "Mesopotamian marshlands" are home to rare wildlife, birds, fish, and the Marsh Arabs, "heirs to the Sumerians and Babylonians."[19] Indeed, we have become one of the dangers the birds must navigate on their spiritual quest.

One of the saddest things I have ever seen is a golden eagle on display in a booth at a powwow outside Lynchburg, Virginia. It had been captured in 1962 in Montana, the sign said, and here it was, forty-five years later, far from the place I had just arrived from—after three plane trips and fifteen hours—the mountains of my home only a dim memory for this bird who perched, huge, dark, hunched, and leaning to the left as if its wing were broken, and perhaps it had been broken. The sky was hot and white as the one eye the eagle had left, the other plucked out— who knows how. *Please, let this one die soon*, I found myself saying. If that eagle were ever sky spirit, it had plummeted to earth, its ankle chained to a wooden stand, never again to fly, as the poor white man who was his keeper said. If energies are angels, there were no angels here, only this robed monk cowering in a postmodern dungeon we have grown to recognize: no windows, no communication with others, no room to turn around. In effect, it was a coffin for the living.

If it is true that we experience ourselves as an echo heard in the rocks, the mountains, the birds, and other human beings, it is also true that we might experience in them our own despair. This keeper of eagles—why did nobody report him? I watched as even children grimaced when they saw the eagle and moved away, on to the dance pavilion where the Native Americans disturbed less, the last of a tribe of fewer than a hundred who gather every year in regalia made of sequins and commercial fur. The allegory grows, complicates. Back in Montana, where this eagle is from, there is a growing anti-Indian movement, fueled by confrontations between the demands of white land-owners and tribal sovereignty on the state's seven reservations. As of 1990, only 55% of people who live on our seven Indian reservations were Native American, mostly due to the poverty that caused them to sell their land to whites.[20] The original inhabitants of this land are crowded into smaller and smaller allotments. In a basket near the ancient eagle, there were four fluffy new chicks. "Eagles, too?" I wondered.

In Montana, at the spring equinox, for the past eight or nine years, I have set off on my own pilgrimage, one I wouldn't hesitate to call spiritual but one without trials and only joy. It is a pilgrimage *to* the birds, the snow geese in particular, who each year arrive from their winter feeding grounds in Sacramento to a long string of lakes west of the Rocky Mountain Front, collectively called Freeze Out Lake, where they stop to rest before their last leg to the Canadian tundra. The drive is long, over two and a half hours, but it is spectacular, past the Front with its peaks blustering with snow even when the rest of the sky is clear. The range is so high and long that it creates its own weather patterns.

This year is the first year there is no snow at Freeze Out Lake on the equinox, evidence, many would say, of global warming. The water is open, a strange blue-green next to the still-bare hills, stubble from the previous year's grazing. Wind off the mountains, though, as usual, is biting cold. The white geese rim the shore as ice would, had it been there, and, until we get close, we aren't sure what we're seeing. Then, the squawking geese protest from a distance. When the thousands of white birds lift off the water where they have been resting, in phalanx after phalanx, one thinks this must be what a miracle looks like.

In November 1995, the snow geese were on their ancient trek to California from the Arctic when they spied the open water of the Berkeley Pit in Butte, Montana, approximately 165 miles south of Freeze Out Lake. The Pit is what we call the 600-acre lake created by twenty years of open pit copper mining. When the mine closed in 1982, and the pumps that had diverted ground water were shut down, the pit began filling with a substance that, according to author and Butte native, Edwin Dobb, was "acidic enough to liquefy a motorboat's steel propeller." [21] Three hundred and forty two snow geese were found dead and floating in the lake over the next few days.

As Dobb makes plain, the snow geese were "instantly canonized as martyrs to copper mining, yet another sacrifice demanded by the gods of extractive industry." Yet he also points out our own complicity in the matter. In its heyday of over fifty years, the pit yielded a third of the copper used in the United States. "You cannot long survive as an environmentalist in Summit Valley," Dobb writes, "without arriving with or coming to a respect for mining and miners, and not only because you may be ostracized but, more important, because it is so transparently hypocritical not to admit your indebtedness." [22] Today, the pit is shut down, but not because we have quit using copper; we have simply started importing it, letting other countries destroy their ecosystems in the process.

One could, of course, write a more contemporary *Conference of the Birds*, with ever increasing dangers to the birds on their pilgrimage—nuclear war that results in the poisoning of food sources, global warming that results in the melting of the polar ice-caps, overpopulation of humans that results in loss of old growth forests and the destruction of aquifers. In fact, birds are already dying in great numbers. According to Scott Weidensaul, author of *Living on the Wind: Across the Hemisphere* with *Migratory Birds*, "Between 1987 and 1996, more than 184,000 birds washed up on the shores of the Salton Sea," a man-made lake caused by run off—laden with pesticides—from Imperial Valley farming.[23] In 1996, 15,000-20,000 Swainson's hawks died on the pampas in Argentina due to pesticide use.[24] In the United States, we have lost half our wetland habitats and most of our native grasslands. And then there are the steel towers we erect to watch television and use our cell phones. Activists, Weidensaul writes, "guess that two million to four million birds are killed in the eastern United States alone" by running into towers during migration.[25] Will the allegory we write be one only of diminishing numbers and despair?

I think of the purpose of pilgrimages, how the departure sets something in motion not only for the pilgrim, that it serves, in addition, a larger purpose. By setting off, one perhaps keeps the seasons or the sun in motion—a way of thinking that privileges rectification, not destruction. I try to imagine a people whose rituals would be designed around the planting of trees for bird shelter, the preservation of riparian zones, spring and fall ceremonies to mark the migrations. I imagine them cheering the birds on as they take off for their winter or summer grounds, planting fields of grain to welcome them back. They might even begin an exchange with the people who live at the other end, and perhaps those in between, with whom they would exchange information on the birds' numbers and their health. In learning this, they might learn, too, of that other people's numbers and health. The birds might tie them to each other. They might, even flying over Iraq.

*Every object is afloat on the processes that created it and will consume it; it can also be read as a symbol of those processes and scrutinized for signs of them. What is present should speak of what is absent.*

—Rebecca Solnit[1]

## Limbs and Wings

They face each other from opposite walls in the High Gallery at the Holter Museum of Art in Helena, Montana, violet and gold—colors of the eastern plains and mountains, where artist Tracy Linder grew up, where she resides now on farmland of her own. The two installations she has created reach out toward each other, or outward, regardless, the way wind reaches out, could be defined by its reaching and its reach. On one side, the branches: a line up. On the other, a splay of wings. And the doubling, sometimes tripling of shadows.

Linder has spoken previously of her work as the making of the invisible visible, and wind could certainly be the bright absentee here: limbs swept from trees, birds swirling into the air, both weather-beaten, weather-shaped. "You do change your posture on the prairie," she says, "you walk with or against the wind." [2] I think of the invisible processes—genetic adaptation to the wind in order to ride it, the evolving aerodynamics of wings—or the pressure from without, what the poet Wallace Stevens called the imagination pressing back against reality—the tree sacrificing its weaker limbs for the growth of the stronger, limbs growing in accordance to the pressures of air.

I am struck by the quietness and the sparseness of these two installations, the noticeable lack of explanation, the utter disappearance of evidence of the human— shovels, tractor tires, produce, items which appear in much of Linder's work. As one is struck when caught suddenly alone in the vast expanses of prairie, no houses, no people to mediate the experience. Given only shape and color, what do we make of it? We are not often asked anymore, in this over-constructed world, to make meaning ourselves, which is to make metaphor, yet that is exactly what this work requires of us.

"*Symbol*," Solnit writes, "comes from the Greek *symbolon:* a broken piece, one half of which signifies the existence of the other, a presence that indicates what is absent; the incompleteness of the presence, but the incompleteness of the absence: symbionts."[3] The wings are violet and blue, as if it were the sky we were seeing through them. They do not feel tangible, but light-rimmed, iridescent in the way color is often merely an effect of the light on faceted feathers. The wings rise up, an assemblage, a collection, inspiring as real birds are in their ability to swirl and not collide. Their long, inelegant shadows overlap above them, as if wings could make shadows on the air. Looking more closely, though, I realize something strange. These birds are *sans body*, *sans beak*, *sans feet*, not feathers floating down, but fleshless wings. The limbs, too, one now notices, have no trunks, no leaves. What can this mean? The forms are here, but without the content that would make them coherent to us. They are isolated not only from their bodies but from the familiar context with which we ordinarily view them—limbs which would lie on the ground project from the blank space of a museum wall. I am actually looking down or am at eye level with the wings. It occurs to me that this work, though suggesting the forms of trees, of bird flight, the natural object, the common gesture, is not a representation at all, that someone has gathered these things, that she has arranged them in this lovely and disturbing way, and that what is missing is what we, the viewers, will make of it.

## II

### The Limbs

*May you keep in your branch's wind your essential friends.*

—René Char[4]

The cast off limbs are parsnip-colored and frayed. They are bright, as if, in gathering them, which Linder does painstakingly, searching for particular shapes or "beautiful curvatures"[5] that catch her eye, she also selected those lit with summer sun. On the wall behind them, the shadow-life of limbs, sometimes two or three of differing shades, increasingly dim, as if marked with a softer and finer brush. The shadows add a different dimension to this installation, a background life, a whispering one must get up close to see. I think of the unending sunlight in eastern Montana, which could be genesis for these shadow plays. In August, Linder says, the grass shadows can be ten feet long. Out her window on the farm, she says, "They are part of my daily vision." [6]

On closer inspection, it is not bark these limbs are sheathed with—and indeed, by the time Linder finds these cast off limbs below the cottonwoods and the elms, they are shorn of bark—but a soft chamois, a kind of doe-skin which is stretched tightly over the limbs and stitched with a kind of sinew, making the limbs seem animal-like and, surprisingly, cared for. Why would anyone take such care, such time, in this age of industrial reproduction, to select each limb, gather the skin around it as if bandaging, as if wrapping a wound? As I move from limb to limb, examining the almost impossibility of this *close work*, as needle work such as this used to be called, how closely the chamois gloves and tends to the curvatures, the nubs and branchings, I begin to wonder about the paths growth itself takes. Why split? Why elbow? Why curve here? Why this decision to meet or stop? I begin to wonder what invisible instructions, inner or outer, the tree—or we—are following, what unseen necessities, or what intelligence.

It could be, of course, the wind. As Linder says, living on the eastern prairies where she has "watched the tree branches form in this tremendously winded zone,"[7] she has also been moved by what each individual tree has endured to survive. And I do notice each branch as individual. A small one, third from the door, two thin limbs forming a crotch as if dancing on air—flung! All exclamation mark! Some are so thick and sutured that they regard me like strange, wounded presences of their own. Indeed, many of the limbs recall ritualistic objects used in ceremonies of healing, the wrapping of eagle feather stems in colored thread, say, or the hide stretched over ceremonial drumsticks and rattles. In a previous statement about these limbs, which Linder began two years ago during a residency at the Ucross Foundation, she states that sewing allowed her time for contemplation, not only of the torn branches, but also of our often alienated relationship to the land.

# III

## The Wings

Almost everyone has a memory of the moment when a large flock of birds is startled and takes off, or decides to land, that up-do or downdraft of tint and gloss, each bird part of an exultant collaboration, subsumed in a choreography bigger than their sum. "Often, I drive truck for local farmers during harvest time," Linder says. "I'll drive corn truck and beet truck. It's also a migratory time. So, as the fields get emptied of the corn, this is when we get the incredible flocks coming in and landing—geese, sparrows—when the earth is fresh."[8] Unlike the growing of limbs, which is time-worn, the moment she is talking about is fleeting, here only once and then gone.

So, too, while the limbs are individuals, the birds here are all the same, as if cast in one mold, one movement, and indeed, literally, they are: the resin in each wing is layered with fiberglass and varying levels of blue and purple dye, cast in open face molds to simulate a dove's wing. Wings like apostrophes, like waves, heading in the same direction across the wall, glint of light off the wingtip—albeit dismembered, partial wings, made of plastic, not feathers, the wild gesture caught, frozen, and the archival remains. I find myself thinking of the bloodied swan wings and strewn feathers on the ground at the lake after hunting season, or more disturbing thoughts of butterflies pinned. What complicates this sense of loss is memory: how difficult it is to separate what something is from what it represents, how difficult it is to simply see.

"I've used translucency a lot throughout my work," Linder says, "the idea that we can see through to a past,"[9] as if memory were behind some curtain, some shroud we peer through, made of resin or glass. Symbol, I would argue, is also a kind of translucency. Our hearts lift with the birds when we see them take flight, some part of that genetic, perhaps—birds are the oldest animals on earth, descended directly from the dinosaurs—some part particular to our particular body and its ties to place. "Not only words and pictures but things tell their stories in a language older than image making or speaking," Solnit writes. "That is, the world itself is a language that speaks to us."[10]

How open this language is to interpretation, to our own acts of connection and memory, for one cannot have metaphor without memory. How openly the world asks us to engage. Bird wing, broken limb: they may conjure any number of experiences, something the art not only has no control over, but requires. It is the transparency of this work that asks this of us: *Stay long enough. See through the glass. What do you find there?* Perhaps this is what departure fundamentally means:

to depart from what is known. As when an artist departs from her subject, the premonition as the limb departs from plan, as birds are startled, then find their fit in air. We could call it elision, as in what is purposely left out. One could also call it leaving room for what is missing.

Linder is known as an artist of the farm and of farm life, her work speaking to issues such as food sustainability, loss of the family farm, the reciprocal relationships necessary to "the survival of both the grass and the flesh."[11] Agriculture: the cultivation of, the caring for the field. These two installations, whose images do not directly refer to the human, broaden this question of reciprocity. The birds, the trees live in worlds of their own without us, yet they are made more and more vulnerable by our lives. In turn, as Linder says, "The trees are part of our agriculture. The birds are part of our agriculture."[12]

# WOMEN AND NATURE

On October 9, 2009, NASA deliberately crashed two unmanned spacecraft into the lunar surface at over 5,000 miles per hour in an attempt to discover, in the huge cloud of debris it generated, signs of water. In the days leading up to the crash, thousands of worried citizens objected. Would it change the tides, disrupt the seasons? Bill Nye, Vice-President of the Planetary Society and the Science Guy on NPR, dismissed them, chuckling that "NASA even got a call from a woman worried that bombing the moon would affect her monthly cycle."

"So, Bill," the interviewer, persisted, "people, obviously, are getting a little extreme about this. But what do we tell people who are worried about unintended consequences?"

"As a science educator, you have to—it's my fault. All right? That we have not impressed on people the moon, although it looks small in the sky, is an enormous, gigantic, very massive thing. And when we hit it with a spacecraft, it's not even the wing of a gnat hitting you in the back of the neck. It's just insignificant. And so I am thoroughly charmed that people don't realize how small a spacecraft is compared to the moon. But this thing is going to make a hole about the size of a swimming pool."[13]

※

Susan Griffin's cultural criticism, beginning with *Women and Nature* in 1977 and continuing with such prize-winning books as *Pornography and Silence, A Chorus of Stones,* and most recently *Wrestling with the Angel of Democracy*, examines and analyzes life for not only women and nature, but all of us under patriarchy. In *Women in Nature*, she introduces a radical method she has hence relied on, one in which she juxtaposes the voice of science, or what she calls civilized man, with its insistence on fact and authority, with the voices of all those others it has separated from itself: man from woman, humanity from nature, thinking from feeling, object from its subject, soul from the body. "One of the loudest complaints which this book makes about patriarchal thought," Griffin writes, "is that it claims to be objective, and separated from emotion."[14]

*Women and Nature.* The news coming in thirty years ago was not good. It has increasingly become less so. Currently, there are approximately 1,000 to 1,100 species of birds and mammals that are facing extinction. If invertebrates and plants are included, the total number of species in imminent danger is around 20,000. Women aren't faring much better. A hospital has just been built in the Congo to deal with the trauma of the thousands of women raped in that country's civil war. Here in the United States, one in six women has been raped. In Ukraine, Cambodia, Ghana, thousands of young girls are sold into sexual slavery.

Ezra Pound writes that there is the art of diagnosis and the art of cure, both of which, he felt, were "not in mutual opposition,"[15] and yet diagnosis—the *gnosis* or knowledge of what is wrong divided from the body's cure—though important as a first step, can often leave us feeling overwhelmed and hopeless. Griffin, in a 1981 essay, claims her own dialectic. "The voice of despair," she writes, "arrives as a kind of terror. I am certain before I begin writing a piece that I will not be able to put sentences together, or worse, that all I have to say has been said before, that there is no purpose, that there is no intrinsic authority to my own words."[16] It is a voice that tells us words cannot change the world and, regardless, there is not enough time.

What counters the voice of despair Griffin names the voice of poetry. "So much is sacrificed," she says, "in this civilization in which I write, to the engine God of despair. But still, the other voice, the intuitive, returns, like grass forcing its way through concrete."[17] If, despite the power of the voice of despair, we believe in the power of the written or spoken word to effect change, how might we use it to access that other voice? Griffin writes, "In the process of writing I found that I could best discover my insights about the logic of civilized man by going underneath logic, that is by writing associatively, and thus enlisting my intuition, or uncivilized self."[18] According to Webster's *New World Dictionary*, intuition is a direct knowing or learning of something without the conscious use of reasoning, akin to instinct, what the body knows and acts on without the mediation of logical thought. It is something we share with the birds that turn from their breeding grounds at the slightest shift of temperature or wind, the heliotropism of plants and animals toward or away from the sun. It is a tuition that comes from within, a teaching that, because it is ordinarily hidden from view, must, of necessity, be allowed to unfold.

The voice of despair says we cannot learn from plants and animals, let alone the wind or the moon. They do not share our language, nor, it says, our level of consciousness. The voice of despair says that to think so is evidence of magical thinking, irrationality, even madness. Yet listening to the voice of poetry instead of the god of despair, we might feel free to ask, as poet Elizabeth Willis does in her book *Meteoric Flowers*, "What is your tribe and your eminent leafage, your robed rhetorical temperature? Cabbage or ivy or rose."[19] We might find ourselves claiming, as she does, "The treelike nerves to become all things."[20]

Following this thinking has led me to others who think in similar ways, often from other traditions beside the Western one. Henry Corbin, the renowned Sufi scholar, claims, in *Spiritual Body, Celestial Earth*, that the Sufis, in their "visionary recitals," encountered the earth as an angel itself. He writes: "In recapturing the intentions on which the constitution of this universe depend, in which the Earth is represented, mediated, and encountered in the person of its Angel, we discover that it is much less a matter of answering questions concerning essences ('what is it?') than questions concerning persons ('who is it?' or 'to whom does it correspond?') for example, who is the earth? who are the waters, the plants, the mountains? or, to whom do they correspond."[21]

Unlike a philosophy of separation and hierarchy, which permits us to speak for and control the body, as well as the speech, of the subject, to ask *who* is to begin a communication that, to me, seems to mirror the collaboration we are engaged in as beings sharing this earth at the same time and place. Tom Cheetham, speaking of Corbin's work, writes, "This sympathy is at once perceptual and cognitive and requires an attitude toward reality that the modern world has nearly completely forgotten. It is a stance toward reality that gives weight to the display of the image, denying the schism between the inner and outer, the subjective and the objective."[22]

How to begin? The question has led me into a decades-long obsession with what I call the visionary properties of the image and various practices I have learned in order to call them forth. Image: river, aspen, deer, rock. I begin by observing the aspen carefully, at length. I am not talking about mere description, though precise observation, which can take years to learn, is of course one step in attentiveness. I slowly begin to extend that looking and listening and, once I feel I have its attention, invite the image in. I live with it, sometimes for weeks. I sleep with it and sometimes dream about it. I talk to it. If I am lucky, I begin to note it speaking at the edges of my vision, hearing, and feeling. I write about it. Through writing, more of its essence is revealed. "The moment we love an image," the French phenomenologist Gaston Bachelard writes, "it cannot remain the copy of a fact."[23]

The Sufis, according to the Syrian poet Adonis, believed the image was "not just a stylistic form but a vision" that calls for completion, figurative language as a kind of question that propels us toward an answer: "Arab writing describes figurative language as follows: a person will be fascinated by a phrase whose meaning is incomplete and which is represented figuratively, and he will long to complete it. However, if the person reads something whose meaning is instantly clear and which contains no figurative language, then he will no longer wish to know more. For what is known generates a desire for what is not known."[24] The poem is one site where I can engage with and have a conversation with these other voices, where I can "give them voice" by opening the door to a kind of questioning that continues past the initial conversation. An image that is alive, that is allowed the integrity of its aliveness, moves from it to us and back again, mirroring the complexity of human consciousness which is not discrete or limited to the self.

I recognize, in the work of many contemporary poets, similar experiments. Mei-Mei Berssenbrugge, in an interview with Leslie Scalapino, published in *War and Peace: Vision and Text*, says, "I walk every day from the mesa where I live in New Mexico, and I may notice a plant for some reason, because of its beautiful seedpods or the way it shines out with the light behind it. Some would say the plant is calling to me. . . . I try to catch the words passing through my mind, words that are perhaps imagined, but as days pass, I don't think so. I ask the plant to help me with my physical problems. (That seems to be one of the ways plants relate to people.)"[25] Let us see how this plays out in a recent poem-in-progress of hers, entitled "Hello, the Roses":

> The rose communicates instantly with the woman by sight, collapsing its boundaries, and the woman widens her boundaries.
>
> Her 'rate of perception' slows down, because of its complexity.
>
> There is a feeling of touching and being touched, the shadings of color she can sense from touch.
>
> There's an affinity between awareness and blossom.[26]

I recognize in this process something of my own, the *dialogical* situation between human awareness and plant awareness, the flickering back and forth of recognition and response between subjects, and how the field becomes bigger because of it.

"There's an affinity between awareness and blossom." Knowledge begins to bud out of this experience organically, palpably; the poem, in turn, becomes site of the assembling of multiple appearances and apperceptions, of what Berssenbrugge, in the same interview, calls "an energy matrix."[27] In an excerpt from a poem entitled "Glitter," recently published in *Conjunctions*, we see that the creating of the poem *is* the method or practice by which the communication happens. At the same time, the poem takes the form of this revelatory process itself:

> The moment it sees me, the violet grows more deeply purple and luminous to me.

> Its looking collapses violet frequency into a violet in the world, cohering attention and feeling.

> What I perceive as a flower in woods may be the shadow of a flower-being's action in fairyland, a transcendent domain of potentia.

> The transparency I imagine moving through is being through, not actually seen or touched, not the buzzing of a million invisible bees.

> What you call feeling, like connective tissue or vibrating lines between us, represents this vitality, and I prefer the term vitality to time.

> In fairyland, all violets are simultaneous.[28]

The violet has left its consciousness in "fairyland," a term Berssenbrugge uses to call its natural home. The speaker, too, has ventured out of her usual state of mind, not by actually seeing or touching the flower, not by hearing it, but by traveling along the "connective tissue or vibrating lines between us." The poet begins with mere observation, but as soon as the violet is isolated, recognized, and named, it is changed by its being seen. "The violet looking back, loses objectivity, and enters the expansion of recognized things," she writes earlier in the poem. Its consciousness unfolds as the seer's does. Both bodies expand into the space made by seeing into *seeing-more*. Maurice Merleau-Ponty, in his well-known essay "Eye and Mind," writes that what we sense as body is an "intertwining of vision and movement."[29] For human beings, the enigma of consciousness "derives from the fact that my body simultaneously sees and is seen. That which looks at all things can also look at itself and recognize, in what it sees, the 'other side' of its power of looking."[30] For Berssenbrugge, the violet and the rose also move out from their solitude into what Merleau-Ponty calls a "strange system of exchanges."

❈

In Brenda Hillman's new book *Practical Water*, she writes of her own experience with this matrix of energies. This, from the beginning of a long poem entitled "Reportorial Poetry, Trance, and Activism":

> Experience crosses over with that which is outside experience; the unknown receives this information as an aquifer receives replenishing rain. Meditative states can be used to cross material boundaries, to allow you to be in several places at once, such as Congress & ancient Babylon.[31]

In another poem, "In a House Subcommittee on Electronic Surveillance," the narrator, sitting in as a member of the women's anti-war group Codepink, finds that the voices of despair, the "steady voices" of Congress-speak, elicit from her a certain panic. The voice of poetry, here manifest as an act of creative imagination, comes in to save her. She writes, "It would be lovely to ask water to investigate domestic spying so I put myself in a trance right here in Congress holding a bottle of $H_2O$," and thus, she begins to follow the water's own motions as she imagines it escaping its bottle, crashing to the floor, trickling through the carpet to find the underground vaults where, past the secrets and lies of an administration spying on its own citizenry, the water interviews the ants, interviews (is not an *inter-view* synonymous with *in-sight* or *in-tuition*?) the ferret, enlarging her understanding, which hitherto had been merely human, and "Perspective is gained."[32]

It is perspective that has agency here, not the singular person who perceives. Perspective *is* gained. "More perception had to be, began to be," Hillman writes in the poem, "In a Senate Armed Services Hearing," as she first listens "as a woman" to the Senators debating the upcoming invasion of Iraq, then "as a fly" buzzing around the room, "making its for-sure-maybe algebra cloud" in the chamber, then "as a thought" thinking, and as a molecule on the rim of the Senators' glasses.[33] How *one* sees is only partial. Here, with the heightened perspective of multiple views, the entire room seems to react to the logic of these men, (with the addition of then

Senator Hilary Clinton) who talk of war dispassionately, thinking of their kids, their "folks with cancer," their personal quotidian lives, while plotting—the whole room feels it, even the carpeting—the "soon-to-be-smashed goddess in Babylon." Multiple viewpoints—human and otherwise—enlarge our understanding of the depth and consequence of events and enlarge the field of possible solutions. When we ask who is the fly are we not asking from what perspective does it see? Is not the answer to who is the fly the particular set of perceptions it embodies? We cannot know *except through* imagination: the simile of the life force that connects each to each, the metaphor that floods past the boundaries of self. The fly, like the woman, is an outsider, is not sure, does not believe in one answer because one answer precludes the answers of all the others.

"It is nearly impossible to think about" leading a moral life, Hillman writes in the title poem, "Practical Water."[34] It feels so especially now, particularly if one is an American. Given the enormity of our position (our responsibility for war, for recent tortures, for the Gulf filling with oil, the rapid extinction of species), the double-meaning of the phrase—*It is nearly impossible to think about*—hits home. We not only can't think about it because the situation is cause for shame and despair; we can't rely on only thinking as a way out of it. It won't work. What will? "An ethics occurs at the edge / of what we know," Hillman writes. Where is that edge? "The creek goes underground about here," she writes. As the subterranean mind we share with water, and consequently, with all living things that depend on it, the image of the underground creek is at the same time both literal and figurative, by which I mean tied inexorably to our own lives. How to live the moral life? "You should make yourself uncomfortable / If not you who." Again, here are multiple meanings. If you are uncomfortable, it is because you are out of your element, which has been posited on your own ease in the world. If you are not this set of comforts, who are you? Or, inversely, does not your existent comfort depend on the sacrifices of others whom you are blind to, i.e. if you are not made uncomfortable, who is? This seems an apt definition of the moral life, to be unto others, as to oneself, including the water, the earthworms, the fly. "I'm sick of irony," Hillman shouts in another poem. "Everything feels everything."[35]

The ability to "feel" everything is, according to this poet, a power that is counter to the power of the Senate Subcommittee, the laws, codes, wars of our materialist and capitalist culture. Emotion, Griffin reminds us, is what the voice of patriarchy claims to be free of, what women have often been denigrated for having too much of. Here, it is lauded as an untapped resource, something intrinsic not only to women, but available to all. What is emotion? It is a deep motion within all living bodies. In *Practical Water*, Hillman stands up to the ramparts of "civilized men," armed with her knowledge that there are other ways of knowing and being and that many of them we share with the non-human.

※

Janice N. Harrington begins a recent talk, "The Body and Embodiment of Earth: Reclaiming, Reimagining, and Recognizing the Other in the Poetry of Susan Griffin and Lucille Clifton," by saying, "Among the Luba, of Central African, it is a grave insult not to greet another person. The discourtesy tells someone that he or she does not exist. Being seen by others stabilizes who we are. No others, no self. Without others the self is a ghost."[36] Who is the earth? It is difficult to ask *who*—whether of the earth, the sky, or the rock face dirtied by the side of the road—without thinking in human terms, difficult because we don't know what it is like to *be* something other than human. "Who are you?" we ask each other and speak of families, homes. *I am that which sees as others like me see. I am how I see things.* Peoples have often spoken of the earth as female—Mother Earth, the goddess Gaia—but when we do so, how do we see her? In her analysis of Lucille Clifton's poem, "the earth is a living thing," Harrington claims that it is not only women who are often equated with nature and thus, rendered invisible by the patriarchy, but often non-white peoples as well, particularly black people. Do we see the earth mother as white or black?

In Clifton's poem, the earth is imagined, stanza by stanza, as having multiple bodies, multiple manifestations, all of which have blackness in common: a black bear, a black hawk, a black fish, coal holding in its belly a diamond. These are images of an earth that is not primarily female or even human, yet when it is human, its form is nothing like what has been mythologized. The earth, here

> is a black and living thing
> is a favorite child
> of the universe
> feel her rolling her hand
> in its kinky hair
> feel her brushing it clean[37]

As Harrington says, it is the blackness that Clifton wants us to recognize and acknowledge as familiar, as our familiar: "The earth is not only black and feminine, it is a favored child, lauded above others and attended to, given gifts . . . If the earth has the body of a black girl-child, then blackness is also worthy, filled with potential, and proof of the fecundity and unity of the universe." In turn, only when we respect and care for the most maligned, most vulnerable, most unacknowledged of us— by virtue of being black in a racist society, a girl in patriarchy—will we learn to value the earth.

An untitled poem that serves as frontispiece to the new anthology *Black Nature: Two Hundred Years of African American Poetry* (in which both these Clifton poems appear) reveals the poet's relationship to the natural image and the active role it plays in her poetic process:

> surely i am able to write poems
> celebrating grass and how the blue
> in the sky can flow green or red
> and the waters lean against the
> chesapeake shore like a familiar
> poems about nature and landscape
> surely   but whenever i begin
> "the trees wave their knotted branches
> and . . ."   why
> is there under that poem always
> an other poem?

Poems that celebrate are poems sure of what they are doing. They usually are descriptive poems, poems that don't ask questions because the answer is already formulated. Nature, a praise poem tells us, is beautiful. The word "surely" is repeated twice. A nature poem is something anyone surely can write because we have agreed on a stance toward nature that is objective, that separates us from it. We describe from across our distance. But the poem that listens to the tree is not sure. It begins in doubt, as Clifton's poem does. That first "surely," by its very insistence on the obvious, suggests its opposite. Why, we wonder, does this speaker doubt that she is as capable as other poets? What makes her different? Notice the line break between "familiar" and "poems." A familiar is a family member, recognizable, also a kind of guide, someone who accompanies us and teaches us about ourselves. At the same time, Clifton seems to be making a point about "familiar poems about nature" which objectify by merely describing.

"The trees wave their knotted branches," she begins her description and then is lost. The tree has asserted something. It waves, as if to get her attention. It is not waved, or made to wave, for instance, by the wind. The image stops the typical progression, then suddenly leads her down a different, darker road. What is knotted? A branch? Or a rope? Are the branches knotted because a rope is tied around them? What is knotted in them? It is the image itself that opens these questions. (Again, Adonis: "Since figurative language is ambiguous, it does not provide any conclusive answers. It is, in fact, a battleground on which the struggle over contradictory meanings is played out. Figurative language only raises more questions."[38]) The poet doubts. She realizes that the poem she had started out to write is not the poem being written. The poem collapses into something new. There is something under the poem and something under the tree that she has been avoiding. What? We realize that the poem was strange from the very beginning, though we kept reading, sure of a different outcome: "how the blue / in the sky can flow green or red." After the startling disclosure at the end, enigmatic as the image is, we are led back to the beginning. How does blue flow green? Perhaps it is the color behind the blue, a painter's back-color, a trick of light? Or is it green that flows up to blue, as in a tree, or blood, which is red flowing, that flows down?

Of course, what is under the conventional nature poem is here contextualized by race. Lucille Clifton is a black woman. We would read this poem differently if we didn't know that, if we didn't know she were American; rather, we wouldn't understand it. This is the knowledge she brings to us, as well as the knowledge the tree brought to her. There is always, the poet writes, another voice under our voice, calling. Perhaps that is why poetry seems intrinsically and eminently capable of doing this work of making unstable the boundaries of the self, whether the voice that answers speaks of its own life or that of others who are connected to it, in this case, the dead. The voice of poetry, whose job is to connect, reaches out here to the tree and finds kin, kin perhaps who have been lynched on these very branches. The other poem is the poem spoken by the other, startling, in direct contrast to the voice that is sure of its lot.

※

In an excerpt from her soon-to-be published memoir *The Turquoise Shelf*, poet, novelist, and artist Leslie Marmon Silko writes about an encounter with the rare grasshoppers that she finds while watering the rain lilies on her patio outside Tucson, Arizona. She notes with close attention their appearance: "Their outer wings were emerald green in the center with peacock green along the edges; the inner wings were hues of magenta red and magenta pink with lacy leaf patterns."[39] In this case, unlike the poets previously mentioned, Silko is moved not to write but rather to sketch and paint the grasshoppers, complicating the "strange system of exchanges," wherein one regards another as well as oneself, and, by writing later about the paintings, initiates a communication that resembles a house of mirrors. The process is intensified as it moves between actual sightings of the grasshoppers, the sketching and painting of them, and the writing, the artwork she begins to make serving as a kind of external glyph of the transformation the image is undergoing in her psyche.

Silko doesn't paint the grasshoppers right away; instead she goes on with another project, the writing of her novel. When she encounters them the next day, they are flimsier, walking "unsteadily as if drunk." She wonders if they have been poisoned, but then remembers that for grasshoppers, "life was the length of summer." The next day, she finds one grasshopper even more atrophied, "'dead' some might say because he didn't move, but he was still brightly colored, so there was life in him yet." Day by day, she is drawn further into a world not her own, and, as she does so, her conception of the grasshopper changes. It is *in the act* of the painting, and the writing, the poet listening intently to the image, drawing the image inside, therefore, that the collaboration occurs. The grasshopper is following her. She begins to see him everywhere. He glares at her. Their desires begin to mix. At first, it is the author who vaguely wants to sketch the grasshopper. Soon, though, the grasshopper is expressing its desires through her: "I realized he wanted a portrait."

She brings the dead grasshopper into her studio to paint it. But this step only leads to another step; one disclosure facilitates another. Soon, she sees a different grasshopper and says, "I knew at once this grasshopper was a messenger from Lord Chapulin." Chapulin is a Mexican, not a Spanish, word for grasshopper. It is a word with Nahuatl and Aztec roots. Lord Chapulin is, thus, the ancient king of the grasshoppers, the spirit of them. The next day, she writes, "Lord Chapulin himself approached me." The image has *metamorphosed* from individual grasshopper to messenger of the god to Lord Chapulin, from literal image to figurative, from the material world to the world of cultural myth, a progression which is mirrored in the move from the realism of the first portraits to the abstraction of the last. (Could we not look at an image as a messenger of the metaphor?) When the grasshopper becomes Chapulin, or messenger from Chapulin, its form on canvas becomes less grasshopper and more human. Its thorax takes on the appearance of a dress; its arms are crossed over its heart; it has a circle belt on, leggings, moccasins. Indeed it resembles a ceremonial tribal dancer.

As in many stories of visionary quest, Silko loses the thread for weeks, intent on the writing of her novel, forgetting her desire to paint the grasshoppers. But the grasshoppers don't have weeks. She notices them staring at the unfinished portraits through her window. When Lord Chapulin finally appears, he scolds her: "Forget about your writing. Paint my portrait." That this is so outside our ordinary way of seeing things is evidenced by how outrageous this story appears. Yet Silko's is a way of knowing that doesn't second-guess itself. Throughout her story, she uses the phrases, "I realized," "I knew at once," "I felt." It is a traditional way of seeing developed in the context of a culture that lives its metaphors, whose reality is conditioned by myth, where insects and animals carry messages from the divine to us and where we, possibly, send messages back. It is what Griffin has called, "an approach [to reality] that posits consciousness as part of nature, an experience of knowledge as intimacy rather than power."[40] What do the grasshoppers ultimately have to say to Silko? They reaffirm her intuition, keep her on the path she has begun with them, which is a creative path, one of collaborative vision with the forms of life that surround her. "Get to work," they say.

❊

Last night, the moon shone for just one moment in my window and I happened to wake just then to look at it. In my half-sleep, I admired the sensitivity of my own responsiveness rather than the fact that its light might have woken me. This is how it works, I remember thinking, the moon reaches out just this far, I reach, too, and our consciousnesses meet, making of this space something new. And then the moon faded behind the clouds again, into what Berssenbrugge called the "fairyland" of its own consciousness, as I did mine. It felt as if we had both woken and slept at the same time. Women's capacities have been "infinitely diminished under patriarchy," the late Mary Daly said.[41] The moon's battered spine and peeling pages. Yet that is the voice of despair talking—true, but like all truths, only partially true. One lifetime is not enough for any of us—men, women, black, white—to know a place. Fortunately we have multiple readings of the moon. "Instead of the image of one God controlling creation or the picture of existence as random and mindless, it is possible to imagine a collaborative intelligence shaping form, event, circumstance, consequence, life. By this shift in perception one is no longer placed in an alien environment. Instead, in and through existence, one enters community,"[42] Griffin writes in a later book, *The Eros of Everyday Life*, but, I would argue, it is the underlying message of all her work.

# GOD-STEP AT THE MARGINS OF THOUGHT

My grandparents, tenant farmers in Indiana, with scant education, used to hold séances in their home in the 1930s and '40s. The medium, whom we called Aunt Millie, though she was of no relation, traveled to different farm communities, plying her trade, until she had enough followers to open up her own Spiritualist Church. My mother, having evidenced a talent for sensitivity to the spirits while quite young, was in training to be a medium when she met my father, a lapsed Catholic, and consequently abandoned all those plans. However, she never abandoned the point of view that the ordinary person, not the acolyte, could see things, hear things, and smell things that simply weren't there.

We had "visitors," a host of beings watching over us, anticipating mistakes, rewarding right moves. Clocks stopped, watches fell off our wrists, voices came out of nowhere signaling their equivalents of yes and no, stop and go, and birds or animals singled us out for special attention. Events became metaphors one could find everywhere if one just looked for them. Robert Duncan, who grew up in a Theosophist household (what I call the rich and college cousins of the Spiritualists), wrote about his occult upbringing in an essay entitled "The Truth and Life of Myth": "For my parents, the truth of things was esoteric (locked inside) or occult (masked by the apparent), and one needed a 'lost key' to piece out the cryptogram of who wrote Shakespeare or who created the universe and what his real message was."[1] The lost key, for my mother, was time. She trusted in revelation. Hence, my brother and sister and I grew up with the idea that the world was much larger and more mysterious than it appeared on the surface, that life was a theater of images, a dramaturgy, a minute by minute visionary recital. Her role, and ours, she taught us, was in waiting for the meaning to unfold.

Not that any of her children were ready to become mediums ourselves. When I was young, I felt skeptical about Spiritualism, an attitude I inherited from my father, but also a reaction to the soupcon of rot and mold and Victorian dirtiness that, of course, originated in Spiritualism's preoccupation with speaking to the dead. Perhaps this was a class issue, too, since the people who went to the Spiritualist church where my mother went were poor, with little education, like my grandparents. They weren't, like Duncan's parents and aunts, members of a Hermetic Brotherhood or studying astrology, theosophy, or Emanuel Swedenborg. They didn't have time to read anything, even the Bible. They were tenant farmers, bar owners, waitresses, and cooks. The dead, too, seemed to live on the black or Polish side of town, old women with doilies and a soiled laundry basket of problems and advice. The dead, not the spirits. Why disturb them? And yet I was taught, in my family, to anticipate their arrival as valuable, as having something to teach us.

The last time I saw Aunt Millie I was back in Indiana visiting relatives, and my grandfather was dying, though no one knew it but her. We sat in her Victorian house in Michigan City with its many rooms, smell of moth balls and sound of the clanging radiators. She was getting old by then, in her late seventies, fifty years older than me. She held my hands and closed her eyes, those hands I so clearly remember because they were like my grandmother's. I do not think people have hands like that anymore, small and scrubbed raw from hot water and plain work. She talked about the gift of mediumship, saying that many people can receive messages from *the other world*, as she called it, but that what made someone a medium was the skill one used to interpret them. She said that when she tried to interfere, read into the image, instead of conveying it precisely as she saw it to the client, letting him or her decide on his or her own interpretation, it rang false and the image itself would waver. It was not, then, simply a matter of trust in revelation. It was a practice of seeing, and conveying, in language, what she saw. I remember thinking, even then, when I was just beginning to write poems, that what she was telling me of her own education as a medium would be important in my own education as a poet, that her pitfalls and revelations would come to be mirrored in my own practice, her understanding part of a poetics of the visionary figure itself.

> *The light foot hears you and the brightness begins*
> god-step at the margins of thought
> quick adulterous tread at the heart

"Who goes there?" Robert Duncan asks after these first lines of "Poem Beginning with a Line by Pindar."[2] Indeed, inspiration itself—that "god-step"—has been conceived as an otherworldly figure: the Muse, whether of history, music, or epic poetry, who is female, and the guide, such as Virgil was for Dante, who is male. One meets these figures in the beginning of any classical text, invoked as a source and a blessing. Classical poetry is replete with gods who take human form, and transform, who are appealed to, invoked, whose stories contribute to one plane or plotline of epic poetry. Then, there is the great tradition of persona poems wherein the writer takes on the attributes of a character from mythology or history and speaks from that point of view. One thinks of Robert Browning's dramatic monologues, of Anne Sexton's *Transformations* of characters from fairy tales, of Olga Broumas speaking as the female gods of her Greek homeland in *Beginning with O*. There are also those poems which sound multiple voicings of characters who range widely across time and space, Ezra Pound's *Cantos,* for instance, which juxtaposes and repeats the words of Homer, Hesiod, Confucius, and the troubadour poets, arranging them into what scholar Aaron Parrett calls "stacked harmonies."[3] What we find in these kinds of poems is not mediumship, per se, but an intentional imagining, a *sympathy with* another person or persons.

In this essay, I want to look at three separate books of poems wherein the poet claims the experience of seeing or hearing a figure from outside the realm of daily reality, whether that figure is historical, mythical, or ancestral: the modernist poet H.D.'s *Hermetic Definition,*[4] the contemporary American poet Christopher Howell's *Though Silence: The Ling Wei Texts,*[5] and, also contemporary, the Caribbean poet Kamau Brathwaite's *Born to Slow Horses.*[6] I will be exploring the very different ways in which otherworldly figures are manifested in their poetries, what message these figures bring, and what value that message has for both poet and reader.

> How does the Message reach me?
> do thoughts fly like the Word
> of the goddess? a whisper—[7]

In 1920, while recovering from a flu that almost killed her and the precarious birth of her daughter Perdita, H.D. witnessed a series of visions on the wall of an apartment on the island of Corfu, Greece, where her lover Bryher had taken her to recover. "It was late afternoon," she writes. "I saw a dim shape forming on the wall between the foot of the bed and the wash-stand."[8] She thought, at first, that the images were shadows but realized soon enough that the sun was gone from that wall. The pictures began with the drawing of a head, a cup, a design of two circles that, in time, she recognized as first a stand for a lamp and then the tripod from Delphi. The images were being drawn in front of her, lines, not as if out of shadow, she says, but as if "cut of light."[9] The last image was of a winged female figure which H.D. called Niké, the goddess of Victory, climbing a ladder. Yet even as she recognized it, she says that she "knew" it did not mean victory in the last war, but the coming of another one. She became frightened, exhausted, and wanted to look away. She says that, if it had not been for Bryher, who said, "go on," she would not have continued.[10]

The vision occurred in Greece in 1920. H.D. would spend the rest of her life pursuing and honing the visionary consciousness set in motion by the "writings on the wall" at Corfu. In her last long poem, *Hermetic Definition*, written in 1960, a year before her death, she had come to identify unapologetically as a prophetess and visionary poet:

> I did not cheat
> nor fake inspiration,
> what I wrote was right then,
>
> augeries, hermetic definition

Adelaide Morris writes that H.D. practiced phanopoeia, a poetic technique used to "summon a being from another world."[11] It is a term Ezra Pound characterized as a "casting of images upon the visual imagination" and said it was one of the ways language is "charged or energized."[12] H.D. used free association and trance techniques to conjure figures in other poems (the angels of each hour in *Sagesse*, the ghosts of Helen of Troy and Achilles in *Winter Love* and *Helen in Egypt*), but increasingly she began to see ordinary human figures as hermetic figures themselves, messengers with hidden knowledge of the divine, "bearers of secret wisdom,"[13] as she called them in *Trilogy*, "companions of the flame."[14] Every chance encounter, thus, was a possible soul encounter, enigmatic, charged with mystery and perhaps spiritual meaning. She began to meet her figures not in trance or vision but embodied as real people, fellow initiates into the mysteries, who quickly take on the attributes of myth.

*Hermetic Definition* begins with an address to such an unnamed and mysterious person:

> Why did you come
> to trouble my decline?
> I am old (I was old till you came)

A person has entered her life. *Who goes there?* Why has he come? We, as well as the poet, do not know, although we are made aware of the speaker's response, one that is deeply troubling to her: "the reddest rose unfolds, / (which is ridiculous / in this time, this place, / unseemly, impossible, / even slightly scandalous)." We assume that the trouble is that she has fallen in love and that, in the eyes of others, passion in an older woman is unseemly. (We learn later in the poem that the speaker is seventy, the beloved forty, a fact which is even more "scandalous.") The figure is ancient, mysterious. His eyes are "amber," "Egyptian." He will not eat her salt nor drink her wine, as if he were from some wildly foreign land. He is "new to me, different, / but of an old, old sphere." In trance, in dream—she doesn't say which—she hears voices: the phrase *the reddest rose unfolds*, the name *Asmodel* spoken by the angel Azrael. Thus, a dramaturgy begins, which seems to presage not only a drama of love, but a drama of gnosis:

> is it you?
> is it some thundering pack
> of steers, bulls? is it one?
>
> is it many?
> voices from the past, from the future,
> so far, no further,
>
> now total abasement

Unlike the Spiritualist's, whose job it is to receive messages from the dead and find ways to interpret them, the priestess at Delphi's job was not to interpret but to articulate, to channel the message directly from the gods (though there would always be priests to do the interpreting). As both medium and priestess, as poet, H.D. must do both. How is a seventy year old woman to interpret this sudden being in love (after only two meetings!), her despair at his promising to write and not writing back, her disorienting and passionate response to this encounter? For H.D., the poem becomes the site as well as the method of interpretation. We witness, as the poem unfolds (*the reddest rose unfolds*), her increasing and incremental understanding of the reason for this man's appearance in her life as she desperately reverts back to her old hermetic definitions, lights candles, begs her gods and angels ("and I am temporarily astray; / I can't find Asmodel / in dictionary or reference book"), doubts ("who is he, anyway? / angels may become devils, / devils may become angels"), rebels ("why didn't you come sooner? / why did you come at all?"), prays and despairs, but above all, knows to keep writing ("it was Venice-Venus (Isis) . . . who ordered, ordained or controlled this," who told her "*write, write or die*").

In effect, the poem's subject is not her encounter with the man himself, but the process of mystical revelation, the *figuring out* of who the figure is and why he is so important to her, which proceeds in fits and starts, with half-truths and clues, which unfolds, as the rose does, in time, which unfolds, for a poet, in language itself:

> I can not step over the horizon;
> I must wait to-day, to-morrow or the day after
> for the answer.

The poem proceeds as intuitive knowledge proceeds, by revelation, by revision, by repetition, by H.D.'s employing of her arsenal of trance, dream, chance overhearing of phrases from poems of her own and those of others, consultations in books of angelology, astrology, the Kabbalah, and by vigilance:

> It was April that we met,
> and once in May;
> I did not realize my state of mind,
>
> my "condition" you might say,
> until August when I wrote,
> *the reddest rose unfolds*

It is as if the entire poem has become a kind of writing on the wall at Corfu.

There are actually two male figures in this poem. The second, also unnamed, is the subject of the second section of the poem, "The Grove of Academe." He is an older poet, we learn, like herself, who functions as antithesis to the fire and destruction of passion. "Your cool laurel," she writes, "the olive silver-green / to compensate or off-set the reddest rose." Sex is gone; there is only poetry, not passionate love but the transcendent, which he serves to remind her of with his lovely lines in French, his talk of the Greeks and their gods, his level-headedness:

> There is nothing visionary
> nor ecstatic here,
> only recognition

she writes, and later, "if I can do nothing else, / at least, I can recognize this / unfathomable, dauntless separation, / this retreat from the world, / that yet holds the world, past, present, in the mind's closed recess." Though the presence of this older man calms her and brings her back to her vocation as poet, it at the same time affirms her own path, one tightly bound to the knowledge that eros and spirituality are twin indications of each other's presence, that "the human equation," though it might entail being "swept in a whirlwind," though it might involve passion and destruction, was also her method of gnosis. In some of the most beautiful passages in the poem, one can see H.D. returned to herself, admitting that the intellectual, calmer poet and she are fellow travelers in that they both write ("it's that you write, / even that I have written"), but what his verse has returned her to is her own difference:

> your phosphorescent inter-play
> of gold-flecked or of rainbow fish
> draws me to the weedy inlet
>
> of my own *promesse*,
> and a rock stark as this,
> and only small crabs
>
> and a crab-net;
> sea-lavender—coriander?
> no, these are camomile-daisies
>
> that I crush as I reach out;
> Arabian-gum fragrance?
> no, that was the amber-beads
>
> on the cherry-bark,
> and the sticky pine-bark,
> and sassafras-bark that we bit on,
>
> and some dusty butter-and-eggs
> (wild snap-dragon)
> in a hot lane;

these are not here,
but I cherish my personal treasures,
now that I discover

how different yours are.

In the last section of *Hermetic Definition*, entitled "Star of Day," the poet discovers that the first male figure, the beloved, has died of a heart attack far away. She learns that, just as she was lighting the candles, he was leaving the earth. An odd tone prevails here, not the shock one would expect, but a calm response, as if his death were a denouement to the quest the poet has been on, as if she were not surprised or had been waiting all along for this to be revealed. It is as if all things had fallen into place—"[death's] hand was on your shoulder, / I was in the way, / I was no partner / to that fellowship, / I had had my day"—and she was returned to her own "way" and he to his small place in it. The news also is interpreted as a kind of paradox. She calls it a birth, not death: "So it was in the winter. . . just as my Christmas candles had burnt out, / that you were born / into a new cycle." She attributes the earlier appearance of the angel Azrael, an angel of birth, to this knowledge, and the fact that it was nine months to the day since she first met him that he died.

What is the message that the dead, or the almost-dead, bring her? She begins to piece things together, since it is over now, she says, this thralldom, this "curious 'condition,'" what she had called early in the poem her "last desperate charge / non-escape." What was her place in this? She says that she now sees that her capacity to be moved by this unnamed man had to be "maintained," that it was "a fire to be sustained," that in some way, it was her task to keep this candle lit—this passion, this writing—as he was on his way to dying, or, in her words, to being born: "the writing was the un-born, / the conception." Does she mean that her vigilance, her lit candles, especially her poems to him, were helping him pass to the other side, that as fellow traveler, initiate in the mysteries, companion of the flame she recognized, her role was to accompany him this far? "What has the word done?" she asks. Does she mean that, old as she is, the spark this man ignited was a gift that reminded her of her still glowing life? The poems in *Hermetic Definition* were finished in September 1960 and comprised the last book H.D. wrote before her death a year later. One wonders whether it was death she saw in the amber eyes of this man who so stirred her, or whether it was the proximity of her own death that she fell in love with. "Now you are born / and it's all over, / will you leave me alone?" she asks. The reddest rose unfolds. "Night brings the day," she admits at the end of the poem. The rose unfolds and then, as we know, as she must have understood only too adequately, the petals fall.

※

Christopher Howell began writing the poems that are collected in *Though Silence: The Ling Wei Texts* in 1975 in Amherst, continued writing them in Fort Collins, on Vashon Island, and in Portland, and published them in 1981. The Ling Wei of the title, we are told early on in the text, is a wandering Chinese poet from the 14th century who appears to Howell as he is wandering, too, along the riverbank of a New England town: "He just came out of a thicket below me, on the far side of the stream and sat down on the bank, relaxed but intent on the beautiful water."

In this initial meeting, there is vision but no speech. Ling Wei appears across the water almost as if a figure in a mirror, a twin. We are told none of the details of appearance, just that the two men both look at each other, and that Ling Wei seems embarrassed "because he knew that I had made him up. And I got a little shy myself then, seeing that he was only a step behind making me up, too." Ling Wei bows toward the speaker, "a little broom-like bow." The speaker tips his hat, a very Western gesture. Up to this point, one could still believe this a quiet passing of strangers, albeit from different cultures; even the speaker's naming of his hitherto unnamed friend ("Ling Wei, as I immediately thought of him") is something one might do in an airport, scripting the names, pasts, relationships of strangers for one's own amusement. But something has now slipped. What is real is no longer a given. A paradox has been set up, as well as a playfulness. It is the playfulness, I think—which is reminiscent of the playfulness in the un-answerability of Buddhist koans—that convinces us to suspend our disbelief.

The third time they run into each other, Ling Wei speaks: "Isn't snow a moonlight caught in the skull?" We learn all this in the first piece of the book, entitled "Introduction: A Reverie." That this introduction is written in prose, i.e. the language of discourse, of explanation, suggests that what we are going to be told is factual—*this is how I came to write this book*—and indeed, the tone is matter-of-fact, though lyrical, too, speaking as it does of the loveliness of the turning seasons. Prose also suggests that there is a narrative, a time before the meeting of Ling Wei and a time after, that follows the conventions of chronological and seasonal time. As soon as Ling Wei speaks his decidedly poetic and somewhat cryptic words, however, everything we assumed about the speaker's conventionality is cast into doubt. And yet, the speaker continues as if what he were saying is not improbable. The speaker thanks Ling Wei for the metaphor: "it was exactly right; everything looked like the moon made me feel." We are told that Ling Wei spoke to him often after that, "in Chinese (with English subtitles)" and we learn here, for the first time, that Ling Wei has now gone back "to the 14th century" where, we are asked to believe, he came from. Why Chinese? Why 14th century? Howell leaves those questions alone as if to say: because that is who came. We learn that the figure is a poet like the speaker. We will learn from the poems that he is lonely, in exile. We already know, from the introduction, that the speaker is alone, perhaps lonely, and in some kind of exile, too—at least from normative relations in time. They are both walkers and widely wandering. How did they find each other and why?

The second piece in the book is a poem entitled "Pre-Epilogue," the title itself a contradiction and an inversion of traditional narrative. One expects an epilogue at the end of a book. One expects that that is where we will learn what happened after the work was finished, that we will learn the answers to some of these questions. But here, the voice of disclosure is replaced with one of doubt:

> You have written it
> yourself, a blue message
> scratched in ice: 'Beware!
> the secret is two steps away.'
> But you doubt
> the simply robed walker
> who sits among birds
> by the road of another
> century, lost in thought.
> You doubt his narrow
> beard and his speech
> to the assembled ravens.

Who is speaking to whom? The speaker could be addressing us, his readers, our understandable incredulity, our necessary straddling of belief and disbelief. Yet there is information about Ling Wei we do not yet know. We learn about his robe, his beard, his speaking to the birds. This admonition could only be directed at the speaker *by* the speaker, who is speaking in verse now, expressing doubt of what he sees or that he sees it at all. Doubt is the other side of one's capacity for this kind of seeing, one we see in H.D.'s hesitations and backtracking, in her inability to keep looking at the writing on the wall at Corfu until her friend tells her she is there beside her, that she should go on. Doubt, in effect, is the magic opening that allows us to take a chance on belief. That this is confessed in an epilogue—a form for stepping back, for recollection—seems right. It functions as a pre-empting of skepticism for both writer and reader and a provocation to find proof, to go on.

The rest of the book consists of forty-one poems, which are presumably Ling Wei's, whose words are recorded by the speaker. We are no longer told that Ling Wei is speaking or where the transcription takes place. We are not supplied footnotes, as we might have if this were the work of a contemporary translator. There is mention of oxen, lutes, marriage chambers, pavilions, and monks, the truck of 14th century China. There is "The Pass of Three Mists." From the first time he speaks, Ling Wei disappears as a figure. He incarnates solely as voice. Each poem is dreamlike, quiet, distinctly Chinese, as if the poet were inhabiting a moonlit world where people wandered from village to village. There is a beauty and a sadness to Ling Wei's life, and an acute attention to nature, that are reminiscent of Japanese haiku masters like Basho:

> Rain is a gift, astonishing
> the grasses.

One thinks of Ezra Pound's famous adaptation of Li Po's "The River Merchant's Wife: A Letter" wherein a woman misses her husband: "The paired butterflies are already yellow with August / Over the grass in the West garden." It could be the presiding spirit of the poem "Ling Wei Thinks of His Beloved," couched as it is within the reeds and rushes of longing:

> Last night, the Pass of Three
> Mists disappearing behind me,
> I sailed south a lovely boat
> of thoughts for her, a garland of silver
> and blue. But now it has returned, empty
> like this northern season, like hunger
> or a promise to cause pain.

Yet we are aware, in subtle ways, that the speaker hasn't completely disappeared; we feel him in the titling of the poems, in his placing of the figure in context: "Ling Wei in Exile," "Ling Wei Undecided, Looking for Clues," "Ling Wei's Small Song for His Home Valley." There is also something strange, some slippage from ancient Chinese to the contemporary that we feel in the poems themselves. There are metaphors, delightfully unexpected and decidedly un-Chinese: "the cold socket of sleep," "the sky has a blue wrist," "the edges of the city shine like border designs of fine books and jewelry." After dark, the "silver" peacock is "a creature cut whole from the moon." There are mixed metaphors— "the feather of sky into which distance walks hatless"—and surreal images—"The river / into which I am cast, clinkered / with souls of the drowned."

Why Chinese? Why fourteenth century? I think about the visionary tradition, of the visions young Native American men quested after during their fasting or those the Spiritualist mediums heard in trance. The figures, if they were human at all, came from the world of the dead, as I suppose Ling Wei did, to instruct or charge. The messages were often cryptic, to be interpreted, whether by a medicine man or priestess or the seer herself; they appeared in trance or in a dream, not as one sits by a river or walks down an empty street, though all of us would acknowledge that we feel the presence of ghosts in cities, in their ruins, on battlefields, in the running water of mountain streams. What would Howell call his friend Ling Wei? Imaginary? A spirit come to visit from another time? Someone to be analyzed as a projection of his own longing? It is risky, of course, to claim one is speaking in the voice of someone from an entirely different age and culture. There is the risk of cliché, the danger of misappropriation. Yet this is a risk writers are constantly attempting, a translation beyond the boundaries of the self and, hence, some new and other range of perception that opens up in us.

> As to the grand figures in my poems: I suppose I think of them as incarnations of Spiritus Mundi, or perhaps messengers from the Nagual, the Unknown upon which all knowing depends. I am comfortable with the word "soul," for instance; it seems to me it can be made to reach down through what is known into a kind of active darkness. I am comfortable with all manner of gods and forces for the same reason and, hopefully, from the same body of respect. I have not thought too much about this, I suppose because the poetry itself is my way of encountering, investigating it.

—Christopher Howell, letter to author (August 8, 2007)

In "Parable of the Fortune Teller," the only poem written in prose (and, not inconsequently, placed in the very center of the book), a wandering monk has found the famous clairvoyant he was looking for in a village market. She tells him that, in order to partake of her powers, people must purchase some of her fruits or vegetables. The monk is distressed because he has no money. "I shall give you this pepper. . . but you must allow *me* to ask the question," she says, reversing the roles. She then explains that she is going to die the very next day and asks him who will be her successor. "I will," the monk blurts out, surprising himself. The next day, the woman is back at her wares and the monk is back on his journey. But are they? How do we know they have not traded places, if only in their minds? How do we know that the position of wandering monk has not become the position of clairvoyant, that the power has not traveled or been traded? Or that something even more monumental and enigmatic has not occurred? "Fortune has no part in anything," the fortuneteller tells the monk when he first expresses his luck at finding her. "We are simply here."

In his preface to the 1999 re-issue of *Though Silence*, Howell speaks of the book as a collaboration; he speaks of "the wonderful improbability of this persona who once gave me words I could never have found without him." He speaks, in the introduction, of the poems in present tense, as "a thing we make together." Ling Wei has come to him and to us *though silence*, in spite of silence, in spite of the exile of death, into the incarnation of words on a page. The words, therefore, become the *site* where these presences can suddenly *break through* the borders that divide the living and the dead, a place where they can, against all odds, infiltrate our world. In his book *Dominion of the Dead*, Robert Pogue Harrison speculates that our idea of place originated in our need to know where our dead are buried, citing evidence that burial sites have been found that pre-date the first dwellings. We house our dead, first, and then keep them alive in our homes, in our memories, in language itself. In fact, one of Harrison's most striking, albeit obvious, claims is that we literally speak the language of the dead, for the language we speak is that which those who are gone passed onto us.[15] Could we not think, therefore, of the poem as the site of such keeping alive, in fact, as the site of that translation?

Exile: *the prolonged living away from one's people, usually enforced.* One is exiled from one's country by the powers that be, often because of a bid toward freedom, often a bid endangered by speech. We leave each other again and again ("It was not for the sparrow / I left thee . . . I left for the star / which was in my heart / burning.") We will leave this earth in death and be exiled from those who have died already ("Hear the far sandal / ticking river-side pebbles, dim / sound of blood that passes / and comes back.") Persona, apparition, hallucination, vision, ghost, guide: one stays, one is constantly leaving. Yet because of what Ling Wei calls the "magic harnesses" of words, we can—miraculously, magically—sometimes encounter and enlarge one another. In the last poem, Ling Wei addresses his collaborator: "Thank you. / Thank you for my life."

In an interview with Joyelle McSweeney in the literary journal *Rain Taxi*, the Caribbean poet Kamau Brathwaite relates an encounter with the ghost of an ancestral slave woman at his home in CowPastor, Barbados.[16] Told by the government that he will have to abandon his home for a new road to the airport, he had decided to take photos of everything as a kind of memorial. A large spider web sparkling with dew in his garden caught his eye, but each time he looked in the lens, the spider and web disappeared. When he decided to take the photo anyway, the lens "split right across its equator." When he tried another lens, it turned so hot he could barely hold the camera. Baffled but determined, his wife retrieved her "box camera." After the pictures were developed, they were shocked to see that, although two contained images of the spider and web, one shot revealed, unmistakably, a face, the face of a woman he would come to call Namsetoura.

The poem "Namsetoura," which appears in Brathwaite's book *Born to Slow Horses*, does not introduce us to her presence as Howell introduced us to Ling Wei. In fact, there is no introduction at all. The poem begins with a question, addressed to someone or something we can't see, as if the baffling encounter were happening before our eyes, as well as the poet's. It is a question that seems essential and initiatory in this kind of visionary experience, in effect, "who are you?"

> From what far cost of Africa to this brown strip
> of pasture on this coral limestone ridge
> cast up some three miles from the burning sea.
>
>                                        the grave

We, like Brathwaite, have not been prepared for a grave, one which we will learn, in the next lines, is hidden in vegetation, "overgrown," in the poem as well, with the names of plants: "prickly man / peaba, red cordea trees, clammacherry." And yet perhaps we do notice his deliberate misspelling of coast as "cost" and quickly, because of our knowledge of the slaving history in this region, we assume the cost as death and pain. Hence, in four lines, we have traveled a huge trajectory of time and space, from pre-colonial Africa across what must have seemed an endless "burning sea" to an island and, finally, to this unmarked grave, the "ongoing catastrophe" as Brathwaite says in the interview, of "the enormity of slavery and the Middle Passage."

We are not shown the grave, only what covers it, including a spider who "warn[s] me of her entry." Entry is an instructive word. Is she entering our world or is the grave her entry point into another? Graves have always been perceived as sites of such ambiguity, as entries as well as exits, depending on which side of them one stands, as cracks in the wall between the dead and us, the living. In many of the Paleoindian pictographs drawn on the walls of cliffs and caves in the North American West, where I live, "anthropomorphs" will often be drawn as if they had emerged from a crack in the rock surface, the tip of one arm or leg still in touch with it. It is dangerous, many traditions tell us, to stand too close to these entry points. Only the initiated—the shamans, the mystics—are supposed to be able to see through the veil.

In the case of Namsetoura, a spider web alerts the author of her presence but also thwarts him in his trying to take a picture of it. The camera—the poet makes the pun "cameraderie"—is an eye and the eye shatters. It is as if there were a camaraderie between the camera and the web, the web and Namsetoura, to prevent this crossing of natural boundaries between dead and alive, hidden and revealed. The camera, "burrow[s] thru the wave of dark & bring us this," the poem tells us. The photo reveals a one-eyed face staring. Where the other eye might be is what looks like a sun or hole, the glare of the camera's flash. Whoever this being is, she has entered through the lens and become three-dimensional. The poet hears her: "yr silent humming." He smells her: "the musky smell of turning / in yr sweaty bed." He hears "the coir whispering of springs still centuries." The camera has unleashed the spirit of something long buried. The gravesite has, through the means of "cameraderie," become the site of a hierophany.

The Islamic Sufi scholar Henry Corbin speaks, in his book *Avicenna and the Visionary Recital*, of these kinds of sites as being charged by the energy of initiation: "In the beginning, 'Center,' or site of a possible break-through in plane, was applied to any sacred space, that is, any space that had been the scene of a hierophany and so manifested realities (or forces, figures, etc.) that were not of our world, that came from elsewhere and primarily from the sky."[17] According to Brathwaite, one of the practices of Kumina—the most African of the spiritual practices found in his native Jamaica—involves possession by "one of the three classes of Gods—sky, earth-bound, and ancestors [zambies], these last being the most common form of possession." Brathwaite speculates that a million slaves may have died in Barbados, though the government maintains that there is only one graveyard on the island. Even if his estimate is cut in half, the small island would be literally made of the bones of his ancestors from Africa. Any possible ground could be a gravesite.

Does Brathwaite actually see "her-story?" She is one-eyed. She is black. He knows this from the photograph. (As we do: the photo is reproduced on the cover of his book.) Brathwaite's descriptions, however, extend beyond what is represented in the photo. He speaks of someone who has been beaten savagely: "yr sweet mouth bash / & brutalize" and "all down yr neck / along yr coral spine now welt / ing w/ the busha blows / yr back a modern mural / of dis / tress." Is he imagining her through what he knows of history, the gold bangle in her ear, the ring in her nose, the auctioneer's whip? The language is broken, distorted, breaking our reading of it into the discrete, grammatically awkward, stressed syllables of grief. He acknowledges that he can't go back to when she lived, he can't know what she feels: "suns i have nvr known / worlds i can nvr nvr travel / in return." Yet he has returned. He hears her. She begins to speak. And when she speaks, it is in admonition.

Harrison argues that the very definition of being human is to be bound up with the earth, the *humus*, which accordingly means to be bound to the dead who have been buried there. "To be human," he writes, "means to come after those who came before."[18] That this spirit, hitherto unknown to Brathwaite, has begun to talk to him from the grave, is proof of this relationship. She calls him "great great grannbrudda from this other world," reversing the temporal order of generation as if seen from her position on the opposite side of the line we call death. Whether he is bound to her by blood, by race, by country, or by experience, she is calling out to him, naming him as her own. And hence, she admonishes him: her grave has not been properly taken care of. There was no wake, "no calabash or flower on my mound."

Namsetoura has other grievances besides her lack of proper burial. She tells the poet she has been in the grave for 300 years. She blames him for disturbing her sleep by taking pictures of the web, that he has "destroy the ruin of my spiral." It is not the interruption of her spirit journey, nor the lack of a stone marking her grave that is the source of her grievance. It is the neglect of her people, which has failed to keep their history—their dead—alive. "Whether we are conscious of it or not," Harrison writes, "we do the will of the ancestors: our commandments come to us from their realm; their precedents are our law; we submit to their dictates, even when we rebel against them . . . Why this servitude? We have no choice. Only the dead can grant us legitimacy. Left to ourselves we are all bastards."[19]

The dead, in literature as well as through the medium of Spiritualism, often appear with a charge for the living, a mission, a grievance, a challenge for us. We can forget the dead, perhaps especially under the conditions of modernity, which often demand a paving over of the graveyards in the name of "progress," yet we do so, Harrison seems to say, at the cost of our humanity. We do so and hence often lose a sense of who we are or what pain, what struggle, and what oppressions our ancestors have undergone to forge who we are. Namsetoura berates and belittles the poet for simply complaining about his loss of a home due to government seizure of right of way, as if this kind of dispossession were not part and parcel of the history of his people in the New World. "Yu tink they dispossessin yu?" she asks him angrily. "Yu tink yu tall? you tink yu / mmassaccourraaman = rasta." The fact that he has the audacity to be writing a poem about a slave without consulting the dead has her infuriated: "Look wha be, come-a-yu! mirasme buckra broni half-white back. / site buoy. eatin de backra culcha." Brawny half-white backside boy? Eating the background culture? The dead are not easy. They take over. You think you're writing a poem about slaves and look what happens, what you have called in. Suddenly, *they are writing you*. Look, Namsetoura says, now "dah backra backsite chulcha eatin you."

Namsetoura's words, in the poem, are distinguished from the poet's by being centered typographically. Most appear in italics. There are two sections where she speaks a language neither the poet nor the reader understands. She knows he doesn't understand and again, berates him for it: "De caatwhip cut yu tong?" a pun which suggests the damage done not only to the generations of slaves, but to the generations hence. Slavery's whip has cut out any capacity the contemporary poet might have to understand the language of his ancestors. The whip, three centuries of colonialism, genocide—everything that has happened to the people conflates in one line. That Namsetoura speaks in riddles, neologisms, and half-translated dialect, wavy changelings, as if the words were literally traveling through water, should not be surprising. There is, literally, always a translation problem between the dead and the living. (For example, we learn in a later footnote that *bosomtwa* means both sacred and secret language, the female sexual organ, charm, fetish, and a sacred lake and that when Namsetoura says "gye only the redemption of my bosomtwa" she probably means all of these things.)

What is the charge this ancestral ghost has laid at the feet of the poet? How do we keep the dead alive? Harrison believes that it is not enough to provide a burial, that what is needed is to mark the site for such burial—whether one is cremated or placed in the earth does not matter here—by making a place for the dead in our homes, in our words, in our actions, in our bodies, *in our poems*.[20] We honor them and acknowledge them there, what they have suffered, what they have gained for us. We mark their passage here. We give them voice. Because without them, we would literally be nothing. "Gye only the redemption of my bosomtwa, / mi tell yu," Namestoura says to the poet at the end of the poem, "an de chilldren chilldren dis-yah wound / mi seh." You are only the redemption of my legacy, my womb, my sacredness? And the children's children—the future generations—this is your wound? It is her job to tell him: "mi tell yu," "mi seh." The pronouns are unstable, the meaning slippery. How else to speak of pain but in the voice of a people which *cracks* with grief, which confuses and salts and puns and swears and slips into what Brathwaite calls the nationlanguage, the mother tongue, a language which is, naturally, dizzying. Yet the message seems clear. Earlier, she has said, "Write dis in flash before de new red season come." Write it in flesh, in your body, which houses inside it the blood of the ancestors, as well as those who will come after you. Write it fast, in a flash, before more killing comes.

One does not only live in a poem, but by a poem, by its charge (if one has any integrity as a poet at all). One tries to live *up to it*. We do not know if there were other words, not included in the poem, which were given to Brathwaite by Namsetoura. We do know that the words—and the fact that the words were given to him by an ancestor, by the dead—have changed him. In the interview, Brathwaite says that the mission Namsetoura sent him on was that he "should defend her sacred space and [he] should become concerned therefore with the environment, both historically and spiritually, from which she had come." In addition to refusing to cede his land to the government, in addition to standing up for the history of his people by publicizing the political situation in his lectures and his writing, he has been responsible to his vision in a deeper, more intimate, more—to use an expression from Harrison—*humic* way. He has come to know the land of CowPastor in a way that, he says, he never knew it before. He is learning the names and also the nature of the plants, the watershed, the animals, in a way that his ancestors possibly knew them. The trees, consequently, have begun to talk to him. He says, in the interview, that he can hear the sound of their growth. And we can hear the sound of his.

❋

Phanopoeia: the casting of images upon the visual imagination. I have been talking, it is true, about phantoms, the encountering of figures who aren't, in the strict sense, here. Who or what does the casting? The poet, by his or her use of images, both figurative and literal, does the casting for us, the reader. The casting of the image onto the mind of the poet, however, is accomplished *through the medium of language itself*. Ling Wei appears to Howell across the river, but in itself there is nothing remarkable in that. It is when Ling Wei begins to speak that the meaning of his presence for Howell is enacted. Howell says that the poems, though he simply recorded what Ling Wei said, are "things we make together." He notices the poems as foreign, better or bigger, beyond himself anyway, a furthering of himself and his capabilities. As soon as Brathwaite begins writing *about* Namsetoura, another energy takes over and Namsetoura begins to speak through him. He claims the experience was "dizzying." For H.D., it was not until she wrote and re-read what she had written that she was able to reveal the visionary figures completely.

The difference between the mediumship I was witness to as a child and a visionary poetics is, of course, the poetry that is created from the initial encounter. In the Spiritualist tradition, the medium functions as just that, as mediation between the dead and the living. The messages from the dead that came to my Aunt Millie were dependent on the presence of the living relatives in the room, a kind of electrical circuit that needed to be completed. She simply did not receive messages for people who weren't there. In the examples I have given, it is the poetry that serves as both medium and meeting place for the poets and their phantoms; it is language itself which assumes a spectral presence. Literally (think of the science of etymology) our language is informed by the dead. And we, in turn, give the exiled a place to return to.

Sky gods, earth gods, or ancestors, tied to us by blood, by place, by aesthetic sensibility, by eros—what are the soul's ties and why do they differ from person to person? For rivers, for instance, or Chinese poetry, long walking, or the plant world, a predilection for the Greek or for the African? Corbin, in his book *Spiritual Body and Celestial Earth*, writes that the "perception of the Earth Angel will come about in an intermediate universe which is neither that of the Essences of philosophy nor that of the sensory data on which the work of positive science is based but which is a universe of archetypes. *Images, experienced as so many personal presences*" [my italics].[21] The persons-who-are-present or presences-who-take-the-form-of-persons I have been discussing, though they have traveled across great time and distance, seem to exist in a realm somewhere between our philosophies and our sensory experience of life. The encounters poets have with these figures are transformative, creating new ways of envisioning and interpreting their work, as well as, perhaps, providing us with a new perception of social life—the life of ongoing encounters—as a spiritually significant and revelatory adventure.

*Rome is eminent, that great summoning Rome which for us is still only a name but will soon be a thing made of a hundred things, a great shattered vessel out of which so much past seeped into the ground.*

—Rainer Maria Rilke[1]

Below in the piazza, a woman my age with gray streaks in her long black hair is playing an accordion and singing. Little dogs bark, children shout, a man tenderly strokes another man's cheek, while another scrapes a bench across the cobblestones. This morning, we made espresso, then found our way through the throngs to Trevi Fountain and our landlord's shop, where his mother sells scarves and neckties to tourists. We strolled past the Coliseum, ducked into a medieval church to see the mosaics, defied the scooters speeding through traffic lights by the Campidoglio, and threaded our way along the marble slabs lying haphazardly under three Corinthian columns, to the back entrance of the former Jewish ghetto, where we have rented an early Renaissance flat. We do not know, often, what we are seeing, and we are often seeing so much.

"We want to feel ourselves intimate descendants of these isolated, time-lost things," Rilke writes of his first time in Rome, "which scholarship misconceives when it burdens them with names and periods, and admiration misjudges when it perceives in them a specific and determinate beauty."[2] Columns, steps, platforms, walls so large a whole city of slaves had to lift them into place: the city a tribute to stone unlike any we have ever seen in Montana, where we live, not limestone, granite, or basalt but marble dug and quarried out of the earth, processed and shipped across seas, and later carved, sometimes with a map of the extant city. And then, destruction. In the Middle Ages, it is said, dirt rose over the roofs of the Forum and the adjacent temples, so deep it sprouted grass, and cows grazed there.

Like the French and Spanish who had no idea the cave paintings of the early *Homo sapiens* blazed resplendent on cave walls in the nearby mountains, most Romans of the Middle Ages, we read, also did not really see the ruins in their midst. When their town was destroyed in the last years of the empire, they rebuilt, using what materials they could pilfer and recycle, creating another part of town, down the road, going on with their lives, buying bread, walking past the ruins, as Romans do now. Until the Renaissance, few had much interest in the classical world, let alone the wealth they would need to restore it. But did the common people not marvel as we do at the columns crumbling down the road? Did they not wonder how they were related to the people who placed them? Or did they ignore them, like the Roman centurion whose sandal print was found in the painted Neolithic cave of Niaux,[3] incapable of explaining to anyone what was there?

Much has been said of the way the Indians in America did not recognize the explorers who came to invade their land because there was no precedent for such big ships on the water. Rome's ruins are not as old as some of those Native villages— only three thousand years old, close in age to the oldest rock paintings we have been exploring in Montana. How odd to think of shamans painting or carving their inner visions of the nonhuman—deer, sheep, elk, eagles—on rock walls, while in the Mediterranean, slaves were quarrying rock for these grand temples. "Animals are the old language of the imagination; one of the ten thousand tragedies of their disappearance would be a silencing of this speech," writes Rebecca Solnit in *A Field Guide for Getting Lost*.[4] The games held in the Coliseum in 248 A.D. to mark the thousandth anniversary of Rome's founding involved the deaths of hundreds of lions, elephants, hippos, zebras, and elks, imported for the entertainment of the masses. Today, as in most cities, the animals we see are carved in marble: four turtles climbing over the lip of the basin at Piazza Mattei, the bees lapping water near the bus stop in Bernini's little *Fontana delle Api*. We cool our hands in the lightest of aqua waters pouring from the mouths of fishes. We laugh at the cornucopia, huge and phallic, which is often placed in the sea gods' hands, an extinct species surely. And then there are the animals that appear only in stories of place, the she-wolf who suckled the twins Romulus and Remus, the ravens who used to live in the walnut tree at Santa Maria del Popolo, where Nero is buried, who were believed to be demons haunting him for his crimes, so that the people, frightened of the whistles and shrieks at night, cut the tree down.

In addition, there are angels—part human, part bird with their varyingly sized wings. My favorite, in the thirteenth-century frescos at Santa Cecelia, are rainbow colored and individually feathered in a pattern that is chromatic, making them appear multi-petaled like dahlias. The stone angels that flank either side of the entrance to the Fabricio Bridge wear faces so smoothed by the hands of time and rain and wind that they are featureless, what death's hands might accomplish, that extreme weather of death we must survive, so Dante wrote, to get to paradise. "If you had wings," I ask my lover one morning as I rub her thin shoulders, "what would they look like?" "They would be silver and gold," she says, "changing color in different light, and they would hang down to the ground and reach far above me. But I could also retract them so no one would know I have them." If she were an angel, she would be at home here.

✳

I often believe that if we can choose a definite focus, an image, a figure for our journey, we can secure an orientation, as well as a theme. Our first evening in Rome, we find il Tevere—the Tiber—only a block from our flat: slow moving, olive green, dividing in two around its lovely island, la Isola Tiberina, which we walk to over the oldest bridge in the city still in operation, built in 62 B.C. In Rome, the Tiber runs deep below its pavements. The Lungotevere, a street that straddles it on either side, is one of the main bus routes to the Vatican. Yet below, down the steep stone steps we find near every bridge, is a walkway only frequented by the homeless, the junkies, and an occasional jogger, and even those infrequently, so that we are often the only people there. Quiet, shadowed by the steep walls of the embankments and the plane trees above, the world by the river creates its own kind of *garden peace*,[5] as Rilke called it. Along one length, someone has drawn gigantic, exquisite silhouettes of nursing animals on the wall, all with hanging udders: wolves, rabbits, deer, stylized in the Etruscan way. In another stretch, poems, placed on plaques at ten or twelve-foot intervals, bear tribute to the river in both Italian and the native language of the poets: Milosz, Melville, Ciardi, Homer, and Dante. In the weeks that follow, whenever we are lost in the maze and mayhem of city streets, we ask, "*Dov'è il fiume?*" or "*Dov'è il Tevere?*" and people stop for a minute, as if the question were odd—we are not asking directions to a certain ruin, basilica, or street—but they always know where the river is and answer us by pointing.

One morning, we reserve tickets on a riverboat to Ostia Antica, the ancient Roman port used before the river silted up and it became unusable. We walk and run our way under four bridges for an hour, sure we will miss our reservation, but when we arrive ten minutes late, the captain is still waiting for us. Once out of the city, the river is opaque, placid, thick as soup. The willows and birches hide most of its inhabitants, all but the two or three river people who sit and stare out from the banks. One wears a hat made of newspaper. One wears a dirty white T-shirt. Their caches, the caches of the poor, are barely visible in the mud patches between leaves, leaves, which are our beauty markers, here, as anywhere. Fragrance from the camphor trees, wild honeysuckle.

It is a cool October day, with a breeze and sun. Violin light, like the orange varnish the Jews developed for their instruments near Genoa. Rose light, the tula brick of markets. Here, downriver from *il centro storico*, the historical city center, the heron is now Hermit-Saint, striped and cowled, its head tucked into its breast. We debark at the ruins for two hours. Huge slabs of marble lie along the pathways: green, pink, apricot, brown, unsorted and uncarved. Were these the slabs that were rejected? Marble from Egypt, Greece, Africa, and Asia brought to the empire on boats, rough cut by slaves, unloaded here, then sent up the river. Sea light. Frescos of flowers. It is remarkable that we are free to wander through it all, stepping on the black-and-white mosaics that depict the wares of the city's first tradespeople: fish and animals, birds and ships and men laid out in delicate tiny tiles, which are miraculously still here on the floors of what remains of the stalls.

Two teenage girls are so delighted by each other and the place that they take pictures every few minutes, crawling onto the podiums, putting their heads where the broken-off head of the goddess would be, kissing the angels, throwing their arms around the warriors. So many materials! So much that was the earth's! Yet here, at the port, eight hundred years before Christ, the temples, even the theater, are small enough for us to understand, a peasant village. A peasant boat ride to it. "Although the world puts everything on visual display," Italian scholar Robert Pogue Harrison writes in *Gardens: An Essay on the Human Condition*, "overcapitalizing sites and images, it in effect conducts a war on vision—the kind of thoughtful vision, that is, that harmonizes inner gaze and external object." [6] On the way back upriver, the captain keeps slowing and waits for the flocks of feeding seagulls ahead to gather. Then, he honks so that they fly up all at once, creating an arabesque for us. A small pleasure he gives us, a bit shopworn, but it is touching, nonetheless, that he thinks we would not have ever seen seagulls before, or perhaps, that he himself thinks it is beautiful, or even more, that he believes we all might be pleased by the same simple things. No, we are not young like those girls, and in a place like this, more than most places, we feel how the images accumulate and fade and ultimately slip out of time's grasp, and no, we won't be together forever or even like this again. But, we, like them, are taking pictures and laughing.

❀

This morning, we walk to the market at Porta Portese, two bridges down il Tevere, to go to the flea market—piles of used and new clothes, boots, wallets, antiques, music, bicycles, jewelry, the sellers, mostly East Indian, shouting from atop their chairs, "*Bella! Bella! Bella!*"—and what we end up buying are packets of seeds: radicchio, sunflowers, two kinds of basil. And now, exhausted, we have come back to our little flat, which is bisque and cream. To enter, we unlock the heavy double doors. We climb fifty-four steps, the first twenty of white marble, the rest of gray stone. We pass, on the first floor, the sound of parrots. We never pass anyone else in the halls. White couch, which folds into a bed, a table with two chairs, an armoire: we have everything we need, even a sort of privacy we give each other in the afternoons when she sleeps and I write, or read the letters written by another pair of lovers, those of Rilke and Lou Andreas-Salome.

The breezes begin at three or four and enter through our opened shutters. Rilke, wasting years angry at himself for his lack of progress, some of it in Rome, searched long for the tool of his art—"the hammer, my hammer," he calls it, "so that it might become master and grow beyond all noise."[7] From the top of the Campidoglio yesterday, the city was robed in colors almost akin to the paintings in the basilicas, which have faded, mellowed, we say, with time. There were outcries when restorers brought back the original vivid colors in paintings such as Michelangelo's in the Sistine Chapel, outcries from people who had grown fond of the subtle and the dim and thought the new colors garish. Burnt sienna from the mines near Florence. Gold vermillion, perhaps from saffron, the crimson from cochineal, precious as spices and perfumes to these painters. Colors that feel like butter and smell like clay.

At noon and at night, the piazza fills with diners. There are three Kosher restaurants down the street, and il Portico sets up outside our doorway, under umbrellas, at noon and at eight. There is the beautiful Italian language that we hear threaded through everything. There are the strange noises we hear only at night: gargoyles, we tell each other, who cry out when we are almost asleep, an awful complaint, and huge snakes that hiss below in the ruins, and the small, dear stone animals—unicorns, lambs—being eaten by wolves and lions, and the loud whistle from a faraway rooftop. There are the indecipherable paintings in the churches that no amount of Italian could explain: Edwardian women at the annunciation, Jesus, white haired, on the cross. Yet here, at siesta, as Harrison writes, in describing an urban garden he loves, "the commotion seeps in through the trees and makes itself heard in muffled accents, thus rendering the silence relational."[8]

Temple time, *con-templative* time. Lavender afternoon takes us both to her breast. We enter into it from the roar of traffic, into the solitude of trees or that of paintings. When Rilke first moved to Rome, he found a little flat by the Campidoglio but eventually moved into a garden hut in the Villa Borghese. Still, he was restless: "I want to gather myself up out of all distractions, and from everything too quickly applied fetch back what is mine and invest it."[9] Poor Rilke, who demanded such spaciousness, such solitude for his work in order to pull the depth he would become famous for out to the surface, paradoxically searched for it in the largest and loudest of cities—Paris, first, and then Rome. I think, perhaps, it was not so much a peaceful place he was searching for as a place he could *make* peaceful, perhaps as we have made the river or our afternoons such. Indeed, it is not long before Salome receives these words in one of Rilke's letters: "I have swept the heavy pools of rain from my flat rooftop and raked withered oak leaves off to the side and that has made me warm and now, after this little burst of real work, my blood is singing as in a tree. And for the first time in so long I feel the tiniest bit free and festive and as if you might walk into my life."[10]

❋

When the Nazis arrived in Rome in 1943, they gave the Jews thirty hours to collect an obscene amount of gold in order to save the community from deportation. In a film we watch, we see children removing their gold chains, women going into drawers for hidden jewelry and candlesticks, all engaged in this effort to save one another. Two days after they presented the gold, the Germans rounded them up anyway and sent over two thousand to the camps. In the Museo Ebraico di Roma, our guide tells us that the rainbow is the sign of the covenant between God and men and that is why the ceiling is painted with its colors. Across the river, in the Basilica di Santa Cecilia in Trastevere, the Cavallini angels also have rainbow wings. Saddened, rendered voiceless by our visit, we find ourselves walking again along the river. Perhaps even this one, thickened with pollution so that we cannot see its depths, juggling forty or fifty plastic bottles in its whirlpools, and yet still retaining its movement, which is lilting and agile and really quite fast, its shine and even the color of the trees it lifts and carries within as if it had closed its eyes on them—a black Madonna of uncertain age, perhaps a covenant between God and women.

We discover that we can take the public boat up the river from the island, under eight or sometimes eleven of the city's bridges, sometimes all the way to Ponte Duca d'Aosta, an hour's ride, for only one euro. We are often the only ones on it, two women with white-streaked hair, obviously delighted, watching the palazzos and churches pass above us, eating our sandwiches of ciabatta and thin slices of prosciutto and mozzarella, walking, in the ten-minute break at the end of the line, to the red houseboat for caffé macchiato. One looks at the suffering in history, the devices invented to harm and maim and kill, the disease and starvation, and here we are, as if we had escaped them all. This thin slot of peace and prosperity, the size of a life. How it has come to us so completely undeserved.

One wonders sometimes in Italy whether one has dreamt what one has seen, the fantasia of images, such as Michelangelo's *Last Judgment*, humanity swirling, pulled, pushed, driven, cast out, flayed, beheaded, burned at the stake. Every piazza has its stories: Popolo where the first Christians were killed and then where they killed others, the public executions of criminals, who were bludgeoned to death with hammers, churches founded on the sites where martyrs met their deaths, and a god in the middle, in this case, Jesus, grotesquely muscular, judging them all. And where are all the trees in this painting, and animals, living animals, not those decorating the fountains? Rilke writes that his memories of Rome would be of "waters, these clear, exquisite, vivacious waters that enliven its squares; its steps, built on the patterns of falling water."[11] And that is certainly one way of orienting oneself. In fact, before we left, a friend mischievously suggested that we try to take a photo of every fountain in Rome.

Or one might look at halos. In paintings done in the Middle Ages, the halos above the heads of saints and angels, the Madonna, Christ, the Jews who came before him—John the Baptist, Moses—are large, ornate with interior ornamentation, bejeweled like crowns. As the years pass, they diminish in size and affluence, becoming, in the 1500s, a mere ring of Saturn, and then, still less, the shadow of a ring, until Michelangelo does away with them altogether. My favorite halos are those above the Byzantine icons, the Madonna the color of an olive with olive-shaped eyes before she turns fleshy and blonde and ruffled with costume. *O maria, madre della clemenza e della pace.* One afternoon in Rome, we were struck by the rich copper skin of a black-eyed young woman with dyed platinum hair standing on a piece of marble near the Forum, so we decided henceforth that our project would be naming the most beautiful woman of each day, a balance to the masculine posturing of empire. And yet my memories of Rome will not be of halos or fountains or women so much as they will be the figure of this river, which oriented us, and of the light of our siestas, which spoke to us of time.

※

The season has turned. It is only five and too dark to read in the flat. The thousands of birds, which lift from the autumn trees, swirling through the sky at dusk and settling in the limbs, animating them with an almost demon-like buzzing, are already up in the clouds. The brick and marble and plaster appear different now, as if they were in the shadows of a room where a dim lamp burned, not in it, but through a doorway beyond. The day, with its clouds, has performed magic tricks with light, the most spectacular of which is how it swept in and out of the upper windows of the Sistine Chapel this morning, as if it were a god passing through, some pagan god who had long past left this world of men.

I am watching my lover watch the swallows at the window now. The sky is pale as the shards of glass that turn blue over the years on our prairies, just a tint of color on the surface and then the deepness of clear glass, or like the robes of the Madonna we had just seen, now peppered with a moving pattern. Are they stars with wings? Angels? Think of the colors, I have been telling her at night when she cannot sleep: terra cotta wiped over the walls of a palazzo, cinnabar turning past its ripeness. And now, we may add the male and female panels in that ceiling, finely balanced like the seasons: light green shade in the basin of a marble fountain, the folds of a pink robe, blue we might taste on our lips after our walks along the river, gold smeared and layered over our morning sheets, more delicate and potent than any rose. The white of a man's trousers next to the wife's white turban.

Whereas I have been using the word "image" as transformative figure or focus amidst the flux and overload of the sensory world, Harrison, conversely, uses the terms "image" and "appearance," classifying the former as something opaque, stilted, un-open to the gaze. Image is what we recognize, he says, in the photographs of nature at the airport, or perhaps, one might say, in the justly famous figures of Adam and Eve expelled from Eden, or God reaching out with his finger to touch Man's hand. It is appearance that enters us, transforms us. "If we wanted to speak formulaically," Harrison writes, "we could say that human vision in the present age sees primarily images rather than appearances."[12]

The din was deafening in the chapel. Four policemen on the altar periodically shouted in Italian and English for silence and no pictures, and the painfully loud loud-speaker demanded it in many more languages. Immediately, people would quiet, but, as a wave swells toward shore, the sound would rise again to its enormity. We had waited forty-five minutes to enter, in a line that snaked around the corner wall of the Vatican. We had walked up and down steps and through the endless galleries, following the crowd and the signs until we ducked through a door into the large room, filled—it must have been—with at least a thousand people. We found room for two on the wooden bench that circles the periphery and craned our necks toward the ceiling, while everyone else, standing and sitting, did the same.

There are five sibyls, seers, in Michelangelo's ceiling, placed there because they are supposed to have foreseen the birth of Christ: the Libyan, Cumaean, Persian, Etythean, and Delphic. It was the Delphic sibyl who caught our eye first, her blue scarf, like the scarf of the Virgin's, her long hair, her shining green robes, and her muscular arms, huge as a man's. She functioned as both invitation and pivot, her gaze leading us to the next figure, her robe matching green to green. In between the sibyls are figures of the male prophets. Completely yellow people fold their bodies into corners, sulfur colored, so that we wondered if they might be devils. There are the lesser highlights—a book, a child—that we began to point out for each other. For over an hour, we sat on the hard wooden bench as if at a window. *Due donne a la finestra.* The din died away to its lower place among the mortals, and we sat, sharing our delight, while, periodically, the sun would come between clouds and enter the rooms as a kind of wind, sweeping the ceiling, waking the figures, drawing them out into something that reached out to us, as God's hand reached out to Adam's, then exiting, taking with it the lapis and indigo robes. "It is the difference between appearance and image," Harrison writes. "Where the phenomenon does not rise up from penumbral depths, there is no appearance as such but only a static and reified image."[13]

Was it the changing light—diurnal, seasonal, but also minute by minute—that initiated the rising? My lover has opened the shutters. Smell of stewing mushrooms from the café below. "Come here," she says. "Look."

❋

We both wake at six, with a stirring of wind, a few steps on the wet cobblestones below. We immediately decide to spend our last day out of doors, by the river, which is, by now, a brown syrup, but the air is luscious after the storm, is satin. She wears a wool cap and her down vest for the first time. I am wrapped in two sweaters. The sun hasn't quite climbed the clouds, and the stone stairs down to the island are slick with last night's rain and the sour slime of bird droppings.

We stop to watch the cormorants that have perched on the Ponte Rotto, what is left of it an ornate marble slab grown through with green life, built in the first days of Rome. It is All Souls Day, and so we talk of the priestesses who perhaps watched this water from the bridge, of the women hidden under the rubble of this male city. We think, if they had a monument, it would not be a thirty-foot likeness of themselves cast in bronze, it would not be a bust or crypt or pyramid or even a church. It would be overgrown with parsley and violets, moss and fennel. It would be a bridge like this one, in the center of a river, without connection to either side. It would be chalk darkened with dirt and shadow, almost invisible except to those to whom it whispers in its cormorant voice. We walk the island as the sun rises and hope that God is not female or male, but like this bridge, a mystery between us.

One more boat ride. The captain is by now half-charmed by us, again the only people on the boat. We think perhaps it must be subsidized by the city for commuters, but alas, it is too slow and too irregular. Today, for instance, we are informed that it is only going as far as Ponte Cavour, a half hour before we usually debark for the red houseboat and our perfect coffees, and that, unlike other days, we cannot ride it back. The light off the river makes yellow the sand-colored bricks of the buildings above us as we walk the three or four miles home. "Appearances," writes Harrison, "owe their poignancy—their almost unbearable beauty and power of evocation—to the time-boundedness that attunes us to the fleeting moods of nature."[14] Swollen with flood, clear as the skin over one's fingertip held to the sun, the river today is dressed in elm light. Wooden shutters, the traffic above us, the *campanelli* ringing the five o'clock hour: the river and the silence we find here are far older than all this, yet it is, at the same time, *our* river, an experience we have created—contemporary, mysterious, changing daily, hourly, something brought into being by our focus on it. Although Harrison is speaking about gardens when he says, "Nature blossoms forth in a tapestry of soul-penetrating appearances only where human care pervades the picture,"[15] I would also argue that it is not only the building, planting, or designing of the tangible that is our only method of such care; it is our capacity to *attend*.

In the evening, we decide to take a bus to Santa Susanna above the Fontana del Tritone and past our favorite, the tiny, nondescript Bee Fountain, to hear the nuns sing Gregorian chants. Despite the disturbing murals of women covering the walls—Susanna's nakedness violated by the elders, Susanna, the martyr, her head being chopped off—we find the music peaceful. But we leave before the consecration of the host. We had read on a placard that San Bartolomea all'Isola, the church on our little island, was having a procession at six to the river for all the souls who have died in journeys by water, and we don't want to miss it.

Hurrying to get there, we don't validate our tickets, since we have seen no one ever do so, and because we want to use them for our before-dawn trip to the train.

And suddenly, we are in the midst of a drama, the Italian metro police, a stern young man shouting at us to give up our passports and our money, and, finding we have neither, threatening to take us to a Roman jail. For what seems like an hour, we endure his threats and the stares of everyone else on the bus, along with a couple of Americans offering their own validated tickets, and, when the bus doors open at a stop, a beautiful older Italian woman whispering to us hurriedly, "Run!" But, of course, we can't run. Because suddenly, this isn't our city. We don't know anything about it. Do Metro police carry guns? Will he run after us and overtake us? What if we are in jail and cannot make our plane? Finally, the matter is resolved with a large bill and us being kicked off in the midst of a promenade of unspeakable proportions, thousands of people all making their way at dusk to somewhere— we have no idea where—for the holiday. We are in a part of the city we don't recognize. It is dark. "*Dov'è il Tevere?*" we ask.

When we arrive at Ponte Fabricio, we step aside so that the parishioners, led by the priest, can pass us on their way to drop off their candles. We are sad. We have been frightened. And remorseful for creating our own bad scene. And now, we have missed the procession. It is dark, and we can barely see the waves. "No matter," my lover says. "Let's walk one more time by the water." We cross the bridge to descend the steps, and, to our amazement, we are greeted with the sight of hundreds of votives burning on either side of the pathway around the island, like an airport runway, only glittering, as if the stars could be made to line up in order: the river ritualized, we feel, as if for us. We go down, and, once again, we are alone next to the river. The candlelight flecks off the wave tips and, further out, it creates a mosaic of spiraling foliage in blacks and greens.

# THE IMAGINAL BOOK OF CAVE PAINTINGS

Late winter in Montana, well below freezing, but we have come to the drylands anyway, where the views are magnificent and unobstructed to the southern ranges. The brown prairies, rolling like bolts of suede, are dotted with patches of snow that gather on the north-facing sides of the coulees, patches that look, from afar, like small herds of white-furred animals. The mythic snow-deer, we decide to call them. We walk to a ruined homestead where my friend likes to pick around—*poor family, such a hard life*—finding nuggets of glass that age has turned translucent aqua and lavender.

Despite the harshness, the cold and unrelenting wind, there are always unlikely marvels. Today, for instance, we suddenly find ourselves in the midst of a bluebird migration, forty, fifty, maybe a hundred rising into the air, landing on the barbed wire fence, then dropping to the sage and cactus-covered ground. Further down the path, more, that trick wild things play of disappearing into a surface—dun prairie or bare tree—until you see one figure, which enables you to see the many others.

Something brown and large runs across the road, ducks into a ditch. We stare into the dry grass, the forked broken tines of dogwood that look like ears and then, they *are* ears, black tufts of a lynx, up on its haunches to stare back at us. We watch it through binoculars: the green golden eyes, the dramatic black and golden stripes above them, its face the mask of an actor in a Mystery Play.

It is said that even after the reindeer disappeared in parts of Siberia, they still occupied a place in the mythology of the people, who dressed their horses in masks made of leather, fur, and felt and adorned them with life-size antlers.[1] For most people today, an encounter with a wild animal *in the wild* is rare, provoking feelings ranging from fear to awe to a kind of honor that they have been chosen for such disclosure. Even in dreams, animal sightings are felt to be special, symbolic, as if they were ambassadors from some more ancient realm, a realm far deeper than the human. Having lived in Montana for over thirty-five years and never having seen a lynx, an animal nearly eradicated in the eastern United States, I feel the presence of something calling to me beyond my understanding.

On our way home, we encounter a blizzard, a lovely one, each flake so large and distinct that we can see the landscape between them. I am driving and suddenly, something else catches my eye. There are drawings on the rock face of an outcropping of large boulders we are passing. Pictographs? Yes, there is an arrow, a few tally marks, perhaps a figure. What figure? An animal? It is astonishing to me that I haven't seen them before, or that no one else I know has ever mentioned them. Even though this is a backcountry dirt road, people drive by here every day, must have passed them for at least a thousand years. Maybe two. A certain slant of light? That unmistakable rose-orange of hematite against the snow? We get out of the car to look closer. Like the lynx that, running across the road, had caught my eye, this, too, seems to come out of nowhere, as if a door had opened where before there was no door.

❋

According to archaeologist Mavis Ann Loscheider Greer, as of 1995, 626 rock art sites have been recorded in Montana.[2] These sites consist of pictographs (paintings on rock surfaces) and petroglyphs (images that are etched or pecked into the rock). The oldest known pictograph on the western plains is an image of a black-painted turtle on the back wall of Pictograph Cave outside Billings, which produced AMS dates that averaged 2,145 years before present (B.P.).[3] The oldest petroglyph site nearby is in eastern Wyoming, where a hunting scene has been dated as early as 11,300 B.P.[4] The images range from simple hand-prints and finger-marks to elaborate *anthropomorphs* and *zoomorphs*—figures that resemble humans and animals, respectively, but which also display decidedly non-human or non-animal characteristics such as having no arms, or many arms, or no head or the head of a bird or beast. Nested arcs, hand-smears, spatter marks, knotted chains, concentric circles, gargets, hand-held wands, pubic fringes: the rock surfaces house a world of imagery with an archaeological vocabulary all their own.

Montana, of course, is not unique. People have been pecking and painting images into rock all over the world, with Australia having the longest continuous tradition, perhaps over 40,000 years old, and an engraved piece of ochre found in a cave in

South Africa that has been dated to 77,000 B.P.[5] The Paleolithic pictographs that were dramatically discovered by schoolboys in the Lascaux cave in 1940, and in the Chauvet cave in 1994, have been studied extensively. In the Mojave desert, petroglyphs have been found that have been determined with radiocarbon dating to be from 16,500 to 11,200 years old, easily rivaling the antiquity of Lascaux.[6] In California, pictographs have been dated to 14,070 years B.P.[7] Early explorers in America found rock art nationwide. Almost every state has recorded them. Most pictographs and petroglyphs, however, have been found in the west, where our mountains provide dramatic caves, cliffs, rockshelters, and bluffs on which to make the images.

Who made them? The Missouri River corridor was a busy prehistoric travel route. The hunting culture along the Smith River, which flows through central Montana, was at the southern edge of the ice fields and was an active hunting area 12,000 years ago. Consequently, the Smith River has the highest density of recorded sites in the state. Greer says that it is possible that some of the art was made by early Kiowa people, before they were pushed to the south, or by the Salish or Kutenai people of the western part of the state, who used this corridor for buffalo hunting.[8] In different areas, art has been attributed to the Pend d'Oreille, Blackfeet, Crow, or Gros Ventres, though most of these modern tribes, like the Blackfeet, have only been on the plains 400 years. Many tribes say that the rock art was made before their people came to this area. A Blackfeet elder told anthropologists James D. Keyser and Michael A. Klassen that "a well-known Foothills Abstract Tradition site on the upper Sun River was not their doing, but instead had always been known by them to predate their arrival in the area."[9]

What we do know is that people have inhabited the Plains for thousands of years, and yet there is little physical evidence of their presence until recently. We know that some early peoples traveled from Asia and Siberia over the land bridge of the Bering Strait twenty thousand years ago, following what is called the Old North Trail through Canada and down into Montana. That Trail is still visible in places, dry and fragile and isolated as the prairie is, lodge stones and travois marks sunk deep in the long ago mud. "To have gathered from the air a live tradition," Ezra Pound wrote in his *Cantos*, yet he was writing in Europe where the traditions were still alive in the languages spoken around him, in the ruins and cathedrals, cities and roads, rather than something caught on the twigs of aspen, buried under the stones of the creek. Uncannily, though, most people who have lived long in the West can testify to an ancient human presence felt in even the most suburbanized areas, especially so in those places which are, to use a word telling in its connotations, *undeveloped.* It is an apperception of something long absent and yet continuing, a presence murmuring under the surface that we hear in the rustle of cottonwood leaves or the emptiness of the prairie.

Many years ago, I heard an interview with the writer N. Scott Momaday who, when asked his definition of sacred land, said it was land made sacred by the acts performed there. It was land consecrated by human ceremony. Pictographs and petroglyphs are often found not only in the most spectacular settings—steep limestone cliffs rising straight up from a creek crossing, enormous caves whose mouths look out over wide valleys, rock shelters at the confluence of rivers—but are also often located in isolated, even almost inaccessible places. That what is called "rock art" was used to *ceremonialize* these sites is clear. Entire cliffs can be found, washed with red ochre first before any images were drawn on them. There is evidence that people did not live in these places, but rather traveled to them, sometimes carrying pigments mined hundreds of miles away. The amazing fact that these sites are everywhere, that they surround us, and yet few people pay them any mind, that most of the time they exist unprotected, even painted over or scratched with graffiti, makes me think that most modern people see them as we see rocks, trees, animals, and plants—that is, we don't really see them. They recede into the background, the setting against which we live our lives.

Yet like an earthquake rumbling below the surface, like weather or the moon, the fact is that they do exist, that we in the West live here, surrounded, in our canyons and mountains and watersheds by a visionary record, as well as a record of the visionary, that spans thousands of years, perhaps thousands of people. We talk about the *uncovering* of the Paleolithic caves, the *surfacing* of the Dead Sea Scrolls during World War II in a cave in Egypt, and the *discovery* of pictographs in a similar manner. It is instructive to look at the words we use—uncovering, discovering, surfacing, by which we mean found, or revealed. The mysteries that are revealed are essentially the mysteries of those who lived before us, and hence the dead. In fact, instead of the word *undeveloped* we might instead use the word *under-developed* in speaking of these sites, as in an underworld of images—songs, figures, presences—that has developed just below the reality of what we call our time.

The poet Clayton Eschleman speculates, in his book about the European cave paintings, *Juniper Fuse*, that we might think of these discoveries as "a retrieval of depth, of a bottomlessness that is not simply absence but one complexed with hidden presence and invisible connections."[10] That many of these images took generations to be discovered, that they disappeared from any human account and then were found again, makes me think of wisdom surfacing counter to the currents of the upper world. Here in the West, Clovis points—the points on the tips of spears, a hunting tool that predated the use of bow and arrow—surface in fields and dirt roads after each torrential rain. Tipi rings, sweat lodge stones, even medicine wheels emerge after centuries of being buried under soil and dust. A friend is hiking mid-August and feels cool air emanating from an outcropping of limestone. Investigating, he finds a shaft that he drops into, then an opening just large enough to squeeze through. It opens up into a cave whose walls are covered with paintings. When was the last time a human being set foot in this place? Who were they and what were they doing?

❅

We enter Hellgate Canyon, in central Montana, by a dirt road well-traveled by hikers, hunters, and campers, but most especially by rock-climbers who can be found almost every day scaling its steep limestone cliffs. Just before the small creek crosses the road, we stop and park the car, deciding to experience the site the way peoples hundreds of years before us would have seen it. The canyon makes a sharp turn, creating the illusion that its walls have closed, but as we walk further, it opens, and we face a 30- or 40-foot high and 90-foot long rock wall that has been painted orange-red to arm's reach. On top of the red ground, which is pock-marked from fallen spalls, is a powerful and mysterious constellation of images ranging across the entire wall: handprints, dots, finger-smears, a chaotic array of intricate lines and enigmatic groupings that on further inspection are human-like with upraised arms or possible wings or horns. Some figures we think we recognize: a cat's head, a knotted rope, an arrow pointing to a basin. The light changes and, as we stand there, the images fade in and out, an entire world, a ghost-population facing us, then turning to rain-streaks the soft color of strawberries or the flowers we, incidentally, call Indian Paintbrush.

We cross the creek by foot. The forest service has worked to preserve the site, removing most of the graffiti and preventing erosion from the trail, though we notice a pile of human shit and toilet paper near the water and a crazed motorcyclist revs his motor and drives up and down the canyon furiously as if trying to get us to bring our attention back to the 21st century. Close up, the figures again play their tricks with light; some are more distinguishable from the lighter red behind them; some disappear altogether. The creators of these images used "hematite or iron oxide in powder form, combining it with plant juice, blood, urine and animal fat," says local archaeologist Sara Scott.[11] They painted with their fingers, brushes, and sticks. Sometimes they carried the pigment far from their favored deposits or, as in the Missouri River drainage, found it nearby. In Victoria Finlay's book *Color: A Natural History of the Palette*, she speaks of the universal regard for ochre, a word she says originally meant pale yellow but has shifted to the red we think of now: "In Swaziland's Bomvu Ridge (Bomvu means "red" in Zulu) archaeologists have discovered mines that were used at least forty thousand years ago to excavate red and yellow pigments for body painting."[12] Ice Age hominids in Europe used ochre to paint their dead and line their graves, as well as to decorate shelters and figurines. In the West, the varying colors of the red pigment have been used to date pictographs and to categorize them into traditions, an orange and medium red like this color being favored by peoples in the Middle and Late Archaic periods, ca. 5000 to 1000 B.P.[13]

There is a small cave to the right of the cliff, just big enough to lie or sit in, which muffles the roar of the creek as it echoes off the canyon walls, the roar of the wind patrolling its corridors, ever restless wind-snake and the restless water. Here, one can rest one's restlessness. Over there, the small stick figures emerge, chthonic, from the cracks in the cliff and go walking across the horizontal surface, chained at first in lines that seem knotted as they stretch out, and then transformed into humans with wings, with upraised arms. What a spirit might look like if we could see it. Or what spirit might become inside of earth. Scott writes, "Many prehistoric groups viewed the surface of rock cliffs as veils between our world and that of the supernatural. As people penetrated the rock surface with paint affixed to their hands, they entered and interacted with the supernatural world."[14]

The fact is that the paint really does enter into the rock's chemical composition so that it becomes, literally, the rock. "When freshly applied, the pigment stains the rock surface and seeps into microscopic pores by capillary action," say Keyser & Klassen.[15] A mineral skin of silica or calcium oxalate also forms on the rock walls, due to rain washing over their surfaces, so that the painted image, in time, is no longer on or behind the surface, but *is* the surface, and really looks as if it were emerging out of the rock itself. That is why the pictographs last. They have found their way in. They have also, one might say, found their way out. Over and over in my reading I have encountered the idea that the creators of the pictographs believed that the spirits emerged from deep cracks or crevasses in the rock face and, indeed, the evidence seems to point in this direction: a bear whose hind leg appears to be ready to step out from a dark cleft, lines of anthropomorphs streaming out of a natural indentation, starbursts and arrows pointing to a fold.

Much has been said about the way the stags, bison, and aurochs depicted in the European caves take advantage of natural formations in the cave walls, as if the image were actually suggested first by the rock and then coaxed into a clearer depiction by the painters, the possibility that the painters were "touching what was already there."[16] One thinks of the horses at Lascaux, swimming through the waves of darker-colored rock below them. Something more seems at play, though, both in the cave walls of Lascaux and the North American rock art that I have seen, more than the interaction between features of the rock and the imagination of the painter, more than the outlines of shadow and light suggesting images. If, as Scott says, people believed that these were spirits emerging from the cracks, not *representations of spirit*, then the cliff walls are not only records of visionary experience but also sites now capable of disclosing that presence. Not only a place to house the dead but a place for them to appear. Perhaps it is as John Berger imagined it in writing about the Chauvet Cave in France: "When an apparition came to an artist, it came almost invisibly, trailing a distant, unrecognizably vast sound, and he or she found it and traced where it nudged the surface, the facing surface, on which it would now stay visible even when it had withdrawn and gone back into the one." Perhaps the pictograph images are necessarily both, a crossing where the outward force of spirit moving through rock into visibility and the inward movement of the human imagination toward invisibility meet. In the process, it seems, the images would naturally become distorted. Berger continues: "Things happened that later millennia found it hard to understand. A head came without a body. Two heads arrived, one behind the other. A single hind leg chose its body, which already had four legs. Six antlers settled in a single skull."[17]

The pictographs at Hellgate Gulch have been calibrated to range from 1020 to 1360 B.P. and, because of their age, their location, but most especially because of the images painted here—handstreaks, anthropomorphic figures—they have been classified as typical of what is called the Foothills Abstract Tradition, the making of whose images are attributed to shamans, initiates, or those on vision quests.[18] According to oral traditions, the torsos of many of the human-like figures are elongated to indicate that these are spirits or shamans who have squeezed between the cracks in the rocks or have been man-handled or torn apart by the spirits of previous shamans they encountered inside them. In many of these sites, red-painted hands or "spatter clouds" are superimposed on the images or they are scratched into and over with something sharp. The scratching may have been to partake of the power that had been released at this sacred site or it may have been to collect some of the paint to reuse now that it had sacred meaning. The hand smears may have been a way to participate or place oneself in an on-going dialogue with those who had been here before, adding one's own paint to the rock and thus, symbolically joining one's ancestors. A public site such as Hellgate was probably visited by different artists and initiates over centuries, including four or five episodes of site use and "at least a dozen (and probably many more) visits by different artists who added images over many years.[19]

I try to imagine what it might have been like to enter these foothills from the broad and sun-filled valley of the Missouri, to enter the cool and vaulted limestone canyon not knowing what lies ahead, to turn a corner and be confronted by this strange cliff, bloodied and honored with paint that must have been brilliant in its time, a line of spirits proceeding from the rock toward you as if out of the past, each figure surrounded by unreadable but potent signs. Was this the site of a puberty rite, a place young people were taken en mass to introduce them to the mystery and ancientness of the worlds they were born both into and out of? Were they fasting? Were they singing? How else might they have been prepared? There is a possible prefatory spot, a staging area we read about but missed before we entered the canyon. We find it on our way out, a large red arrow pointing toward the site, placed low on a bluff so that one might see it from afar. In the dust below it, we find a thick braid of sweetgrass, dried out but intact, that someone must have left relatively recently. Impossible to imagine what people who were first brought to this cliff felt or saw or heard, what power that simple arrow must have had for those already anticipating something sublime and perhaps terror-filled—that unambiguous sign, the universal hieroglyphic for the word "Enter."

The word *human* comes from *humus*,[20] Robert Pogue Harrison reminds us in his book *Dominion of the Dead*, humus as in soil which is an ongoing amalgamation of what once was alive and is no longer, is rotting and transforming and is on its way to becoming alive—and useful—again. "Just as we are always preceded by our forebears," Harrison writes, "so too the ground in which we lay them to rest has always already received the bones of others—'others' in the most radical sense of the term, including those of other species, many of whom have died on our behalf."[21] Rock, literally, is our oldest form of earth. *Grandfather Rock,* my Cree friends taught me to call it. To be human, one could say, means to *understand* that one comes after those who came before. We stand under that knowledge, transfixed as those long ago initiates must have been, unsure of what to make of our experience but carrying now these images inside us, images which offer us a deeper gaze into this place we, who live here, call our home.

The pictograph at Three Forks is in a rock shelter facing the confluence of three rivers, the Madison, Jefferson, and Gallatin, which form the headwaters of the Missouri. It is a figure so small and faint that, if someone hadn't painted a white square around it, I might have missed it, so small that I could cover it with my hand. It is a simple stickman, or woman, rendered in red ochre, with a circle where her heart should be, a hole or perhaps a shield. There is just enough room under the overhanging cliff for one body to fit horizontally, as if into an envelope. When I lie down in the cool limestone dust to see if there are more paintings, I spot a red arrow on the ceiling above me, so low the artist had only to reach out her hand. The arrow points outward, to the waters.

Outward: emerald, field green, crop green, that full summer green I remember from my childhood in Indiana but which lasts here in the West—with our 16 inches of annual rainfall—for only one or two weeks near solstice. The day is hot, almost 90 degrees, air perfumed with oil of cottonwood and willow. The river is swollen and so are we, sweaty, buggy, bitten, scraped by the rocks and thistle, and my friend Susanne's knee is hurting. We duck back out of the shelter, chased by a swarm of mosquitoes. Susanne is from Portland, an artist, and wondering, I'm sure, why we have stopped here to see this seemingly insignificant image on our way to the memorial celebration in Bozeman of paintings by the modernist painter Gennie DeWeese, who has recently died. Across one channel of the river, an interpretive sign tells us, is a chert mine where prehistoric people found their tools for chipping—chert, which is fine-grained, mostly silica. Chirr: *the sound of whirring insects.* But we have had enough, and we continue our drive to the city.

All afternoon, as we stroll among the hundreds of paintings, perhaps thousands of drawings, that are DeWeese's legacy, which her children have mounted for Montanans to see before they are sold and dispersed to museums, I keep thinking about the small, private rendition back in the rock shelter by the confluence of rivers. DeWeese's paintings are decidedly public, representations of an exterior we would all recognize—trees, clouds, mountains through the seasons, children, a barn—though made more extraordinary, charged as they are with her emotion and individuality. Yet like the pictograph, they, too, are the result of private vision. They, too, are what is left of that vision now that DeWeese is gone. When DeWeese lifted her brush to the canvas, she brought with her the many years she studied at the university, her love of Matisse and DeStahl, a conception of painting grounded in the western tradition, just as this young cave-painter brought to the cave a memory of previous rock art, shield art, the symbols of her people's life on the plains. Is there a difference? DeWeese painted what she saw out her window or within the confines of her home. Allowing for the imagination's rearrangement of furniture to best fit the composition, we can assume that what she painted was truly there, that others could see it, too. Her paintings, thus, are the result of what we might call an encounter with an exterior image, whereas the pictograph is a product of interior vision.

Given the isolated location of the rockshelter, as well as the possible shield-bearing figure, it is categorized as belonging to the Foothills Abstract or the Ceremonial tradition, indicating that it was the site of a vision quest or shamanic ritual that occurred between 1,000 and 2,000 years ago. Because the shelter is small, one assumes the painting was done by an individual and not a group. The vision quest was a ritual most young aboriginal people in America participated in for perhaps thousands of years, a rite that involves spiritual preparation and fasting, going to an isolated site, either rock shelter, cave, hoodoo, or bluff, a site known as a place of revelation, and spending a number of nights and days praying for a guardian spirit to reveal itself. This concept of a guardian spirit is found in almost every Native American tribe.[23] Once the guardian spirit is acquired, it is believed to work with the supplicant, guiding him when he is lost, supplying her with powers of the hunt or warfare or birthing, providing powers of healing and prophesy. It is not "a talent once conferred and thereafter effective, or a vague store of energy to be drawn upon; but rather a highly specific relationship"[24] that is maintained throughout one's life.

Not only men but women and children, according to Native elders, participated in these rites. I try to imagine who painted the image—a shield around the heart—and whether it had been summer, like this, or cooler, in September or October when the aspen leaves were turning yellow and the young woman would need to wrap herself in a blanket at night to stay warm. How long did she stay, fasting, perhaps chanting, waiting for the spirits to come to her? Was she frightened or curious? How far away were her people? And did she paint this figure because she saw it come out of the rock just there or did she use the blank face of the rock to record, after she left her dream or trance, what she had seen inside her mind? The shield is what the warrior stood behind; it held his medicine. So perhaps this was not painted by a woman but by a young man, marking this place as the site where images came out of rock or out of mind to greet the living. And, although the paintings were often images "intended solely for a supernatural audience,"[25] placed in private isolated locations, this painting today gave the vision a house for me to visit.

As a young woman, working as a poet in the schools, I always began a series of lessons with the concept of the sensory image because it is a simple, fundamental method for students to focus on what they see, smell, taste, touch, and hear in the world. It is the most direct way of attending to one's experience. I would ask them to make a list, divided between their five senses, of images they encountered in the day or that gave them great pleasure. *Blue between the trunks of trees on the closer ridge. Must-smell of leaf piles in my yard.* Once, when I was explaining this to a class of second graders in Montana, a Blackfoot student in the front row raised his hand. "White people call them images," he said. "Indians call them visions." There is the literal image: brown leaves still attached to the trees across the river and their murkier reflection in the moving water. There is my reaction to it, which I may or may not include in this complex by making a statement or asking a question. *What makes them hold on in these late winds?* There is the intellectual and emotional complex the reader may have if I let the images alone to speak, as it were, to convey their own message. Does the image have control over its own waters? If so, then perhaps there is an underlying message that the *being* of the image itself wants to convey. Does it convey different messages to different peoples or cultures—what we would refer to as its symbolism—or is meaning more free-floating, a feeling rather, or an individual truth, a spiritual essence? And if one then *dreams* of the leaves? Or if one internalizes the tree and speaks directly *as* it?

Henri Corbin, in his luminous descriptions of the Sufi mystics and their "visionary recitals," writes that, for the Sufis, the image was thought of as "an organ of perception."[26] What was seen, in other words—or smelled or touched or heard, for that matter—functioned as a door or window into a knowledge not previously open to us, much as the organs of the eyes or ears do. "It is not so much the object of vision as the *organ* of vision," he writes, "it is what *shows* the soul, *enables it to see*, the cosmos in which it is."[27] If the image makes possible the concrete translation of a reality which has hitherto been inaccessible to us, if it is acting as eye or ear or nose into those territories, what news does it bring back for us, and how? What I am asking, I suppose, is if there is a fundamental difference between the image that appears on the wall of the cave and the image in the world, the nest in the tree, the cloud in the sky? Or is the difference in how we regard it, whether we keep walking into it or stop at its surface glitter, whether we notice it and move on or decide to live with it, converse with it, *enter into* a relationship. With a vision, one must feel that it has come to you out of the invisible, whether or not one calls it a vision in one's mind or in the meadow; I imagine that most young aboriginal people to whom a vision was given would be hard-pressed to say whether the guardian appeared in a dream or within the confines of the cave or rock shelter where it occurred. We could distinguish between them—the real image vs. the vision—based on the *possibility* of its appearance—impossible that a half-human half-antelope figure would appear in the cave versus a mouse scurrying in—and yet that contingency is entirely culturally determined. Or is the question one of agency? A vision is given to someone. It is bestowed, whereas images—those that make up the sensory, exterior world—range widely, are available to everyone.

When a person went on a vision quest, the guardian spirit that came to him or her was not an apparition in the sense of a hallucination. It was not a dream in the sense that one woke from it. It was what one was waiting for. It was personalized. It came as a kind of herald—or organ of perception, as Corbin calls it—allowing the person *by its very appearance* into a realm not previously known. Whether the image came from inside the mind of the supplicant or from inside the rock itself seems a question less of physics than metaphysics. The "intimate and age-old kinship between the earth and human inwardness,"[28] which Harrison speaks of in his book *Dominion of the Dead*, is not only at issue in these dialectics of inner/outer, hidden/revealed, open/closed, real/unreal, natural/supernatural, but perhaps also in what the second-grader was talking about when he differentiated between image and vision.

The Interior: where is it? On the one hand, one might think of our skin as border, hinge, pivot, or door between self and the world. What is inside is secret; what is outside is revealed. Yet we know that cold penetrates, as do the songs of birds, and that light must travel the retina before we perceive color. We bury our dead, we bury our emotions, sometimes our dreams and our desires, but that does not mean that we have relegated them to non-being. Rather, we often can retrieve them. We contain secret passageways, as the earth does. But what does the earth hide? What would she reveal if we could enter her passageways? "Power," the anthropologist David S. Whitely says, in his book *Art of the Shaman*,[29] "residing in the supernatural underworld spread out, under the mundane surface of the earth, in a web or netlike fashion." Certainly those who went on vision quests believed that the image encountered in the mind or in the cave was a source of power to be used in the exterior world, for warfare, for hunting, for prophesy, for healing. What was the nature of that power?

Keyser and Klassen write that rock art is often described by tribal people as "writings" that, "shifting and changing over time, communicate messages from the spirit realm to living people." This would explain the pilgrimages, sometimes over a thousand years, of generations returning to places like Writing-on-Stone in Alberta, Bear Gulch in central Montana, or Hellgate Gulch, all three large-scale rock walls covered with hundreds of pictographs and petroglyphs, and known to be places of revelation. Sometimes, we know from the oral record, groups of children were left to sleep at the base of the cliffs to see if the images spoke anew to any one of them. Young people were prepared and brought en masse as part of initiation ceremonies. Visitors scraped paint from images and carried it away with them. Though the rock art was made by particular people, probably shamans, in historical time, the initiates came to see these images because they were still alive, still capable of conveying something to those who could see them. They exist in a realm of cyclic time where, Keyser and Klassen speculate, "human actions repeat those of their spirit ancestors." [30]

At Writing-on-Stone, in Alberta, Canada, our guide told us that, for many years, modern Indians thought the spirits painted or pecked the rocks because people who had visions did not discuss them except with their spiritual mentors. Though they often painted their vision on a rock wall near where it appeared, the communication was not for other people; it was a record of what had taken place between a person and the spiritual or underworld dimension they traveled to. According to Keyser and Klassen, these images, which were "manifestations of the medicine powers derived from the vision quest," were, unlike the hundreds of images painted on cliff walls in public and accessible locations, "intended solely for a supernatural audience." [31] Often these sites were said to be protected, not only by their inaccessibility but by "supernatural powers, swarms of insects, and mysterious lights." [32] Even the public sites were thought of as unreadable by the uninitiated and required elaborate preparations before their approach. At Bear Gulch, located in the foothills of the Little Snowy Mountains of central Montana, and considered, with its over 750 figures, one of the most important Ceremonial Tradition rock art sites in the West, fire pits, charcoal, and a buffalo carcass were found near the rock art, evidence of ceremony but not of extended habitation. An initiate is someone who is initiating, beginning, entering into the life of the mysteries of a particular religion or culture. To initiate: to bring into practice or use. What the initiates saw or did at these sites is lost to us, like the petroglyphs and pictographs that retreat into the invisibility of the surface in certain light. What can seem completely clear one day can suddenly disappear in the next visit, as if the images were literally fading before our eyes. A hot July day, full sun, and they go back from where they came, closing their doors behind them. A certain slant of light, gray skies, a bit of electricity in the air, and entire rock faces are suddenly engraved with a cosmology of figures. "You often can't see them in regular light," says Scott, and whether that light is physical or a product of initiation, this speaks to their elusiveness.

I remember the first pictographs I encountered, an experience which haunted me for four years until I decided to begin this study. I was on a float trip with friends on the Smith River in the Little Belt Mountains of central Montana, a wild and scenic river inaccessible by road for the five days we were on it. We had been told where to pull in, where to find the trail, which was dangerously steep, full of shale, frightening. When we scrambled into what is called Indian Cave, we could see below, where we'd floated, the entire river canyon; the drop off was close and straight down. Quietly, we all found our perches inside the cool dark on different ledges. At first, I saw a few animals, eye level, in ochre and charcoal, but as I sat there, *over time*, layers and layers of animals, hoof prints, suns and half-humans began to appear. A deer-person, standing on two legs, armless but with antlers, caught my attention where it had not been a moment before. I do not know what my friends saw, what they carried back with them.

In the biblical tradition, knowledge was intended for everyone; "the strictest secrecy, however, underlay Hermetic revelation," writes Florian Ebeling. "For that reason, unlike the Torah, it was codified not in the letters of the alphabet but in hieroglyphs: from late antiquity to the nineteenth century these pictorial symbols were understood to be a medium of enciphering ideas independent of language, not withstanding that the preserved texts were themselves written in ('translated into') Greek, Latin, or Arabic."[33] This "total hieroglyphic, intuitive way of thinking"[34] was aimed at initiates in the mystery traditions. Could this also be true of pictographs? Are they a form of knowledge, passed down in hieroglyphics to initiates over the course of hundreds of years, hieroglyphs only those in trance are able to decipher?

Most people who are passionate about pictographs feel that, despite the archeological record, they have their own relationship with certain images, as well as their own interpretation. Macie Lunkin, landowner and steward of the Bear Gulch pictographs, told us that she differed a number of times in her interpretation from those of the experts she has invited onto her land. Though she respected their explanations and repeated them, she also intuited a meaning, having grown up with those images on her ranch. *The Rocks Begin to Talk* might be the title of a book on pictographs its acolytes individually write. It seems possible that when they do talk, they have different things to say to different people.

I think of this in relation to poetry, as well as art. Sometimes one has to be initiated to read it. One has to be patient. One must return to it again and again. The image often stays closed. The words, the meanings elude us, as if our language had suddenly become foreign to us. Then, the light shifts and a whole landscape of hoodoos and outcrops begin to talk. What changed? Gaston Bachelard, in his book *The Poetics of Space*, writes that a true image is one that, in order for it to speak to us, must engage our imagination and thus, allow us to "think and dream at the same time." It is not the image we "look at," which stays on the surface of the page or the wall, but the one that penetrates into our lives, reverberates like a voice in a cave, radiates out and into us. One turns image into vision, thus, by inhabiting it. Bachelard calls it, "Living the being of the image." [35] The little pictograph warrior in the rock shelter or the antlered figure in the cave on the Smith River retain the true qualities of an image because they have followed me into the November thickets now bare by the creek, in the cloud figurations of the winter sky, into my imaginings of women who protect their hearts and forked deer-people who are so silent they can disappear. The figure at Bear Gulch they say is a midwife because of her unbraided hair is one I see in the broken, burnt-out stumps of winter. Traveling pictographs, I call them, not something I can describe and thus pin down but something that keeps moving, growing in presence in consort with me. "In the presence of an image that dreams, it must be taken as an invitation to continue the daydream that created it," Bachelard writes. [36] One's medicine, the Native people call this.

※

Of the hundreds of shield-bearing warriors, animals, and geometric signs at Bear Gulch, one image has stayed with me. A thunderbird or, as the archeologists might say, "warrior with bird headdress and extended enhancements," extends its wings across the rock face, each down-stroke, like a feather, each a bit different in style as if made with different tools, as if people had added their own stroke when they came, metaphorically taking the hand of the last person who was there, perhaps last year or maybe a hundred years before, the line of the wing often following the very edge of a layer of limestone, horizontal though wavering, for over fifty feet. Though I cannot make a mark of my own now, nor can I smear my hand in ochre and cover it with paint, nor scratch a bit of its red into a medicine bag for future use, I leave tobacco and wonder. Perhaps the ceremonies that were conducted at these sites, small or large, public or private, do hold the doors open to cyclic time.

Perhaps that was the intention, to heal the division between dead and alive, past and present, image and vision, so that there would always already be prepared sites for initiation, the figures alternating between visibility and invisibility, fading and coming into sharp relief. Perhaps the question of where the image comes from, whether the mind or the rock, whether revealed or hidden, whether interior or exterior is the wrong question, one that proposes only limits to the imagination. "On the surface of being," Bachelard writes, "in that region where being *wants* to be both visible and hidden, the movements of opening and closing are so numerous, so frequently inverted, and so charged with hesitation, that we conclude on the following formula: man is half-open being."[37]

*Joy, joy,*
*joy, joy!*
*I see a little shore spirit,*
*A little aua.*
*I myself am also aua,*
*the shore spirit's namesake,*
*Joy, joy.*

*An Eskimo shaman's song. He repeats it until he bursts into tears.*[38]

Below me, my friend waits in a covey of leaves. She is too frightened of heights to replicate the finger and toe-hold scramble it took for me to enter the cave, though it took us hours climbing on an unmarked trail to get here. Our informant had told us that, approaching this relatively isolated site from far away, the cave looks exactly like a bear's head with open mouth, but we had driven in from the opposite direction. We did see the Lion's Head, after which the area is named, a granite outline that rises up above the slopes of fir and lodgepole pine, resembling a giant cougar's head searching for prey. It is August in Montana, 100 degrees, but inside the cave it is cold enough for my sweatshirt. Far below, I can see the river winding its way down from the many snowy peaks above timberline. Earlier, we had spotted a deer suckling her twins in a hayfield, five Swainson's hawks on the flats, two of them using boulders to learn to fly, a coyote family trotting alongside the road. The rocks were alive in the creek where we had waded, glimmering and purple or green.

People often describe caves as wombs, but a womb pulses with light, blood, and color like the showy, miraculous world below; this is a dead womb, gothic-looking, really, frightening in a way I can't quite put my finger on, as if it were inhabited by the presence of something or someone I can't see but can feel. Mouth of the cave: gaping, toothless, cavernous. Walls of the cave: folds of gray stone. A cold wind, smelling of clay and ash, blows *out* from the back of it, as if it were coming up from other chambers deep inside the earth itself. The floor is so steeply sloped that I am crab-walking toward the interior, which trembles with shadows and is layered with dust fine as chalk and streaked with guano. Waterless, colorless, barren: where crumbling meets an end. It is as if I had climbed into what was left of an extinct world.

A great abandoned nest, possibly an eagle's, built of thick branches and rope, sits on an inner ledge above the mouth. There are further, higher ledges toward the back, closer to the source of the wind. I try to imagine being here alone at night, the clamor of thousands of bat wings as they leave for the hunt, the howl of a wolf, perhaps a bear clambering in, or to be here all day, tremulous with trance and fasting, confronted with all that the mind can conjure, summer thunder perhaps reverberating outside. But I cannot. What I conjure is fear, the enormity of what I don't know, can't perceive, my weakness in the face of the deep and possibly dangerous mysteries of inside-earth. "We have no word for this darkness," Berger writes of the Chauvet Cave. "It is not night and it is not ignorance. . . It is the interior from which everything came."[39] Many caves, it is believed, were once carved out by underground rivers and streams bubbling up from the rock below. To venture into them was indeed to literally enter the thresholds of inner earth. No wonder that the mind fears collapse for lack of recognition of what is found there.

Harrison, recalling the eighteenth century Italian scholar Giambattista Vico, author of the *New Science*, speculates that it was thunder heard above the canopy of the primeval forest that made the first humans "picture" god. Because of the opaque ceiling of leaves, they could not see what was responsible for the terrifying sound of thunder, and so, they imagined it internally. They pictured it "in the aspect of a huge animated body: a body not *seen* but *imagined* as there beyond the treetops."[40] I think of accounts of San rock painters in southern Africa who conceived of a "rain animal" that alternately roared and gently soaked the fields: "The columns of rain that fall from beneath a thunderstorm were called the 'rain's legs,' and the rain was said to walk across the land on these legs."[41] Vico's theory is that the first images in humankind's mind were formed out of an absence of knowing, were generated from unknowing. Harrison writes, "This act of picturing an image within the mind marks, for Vico, the first humanizing event in prehistory."[42] In other words, one of the attributes that distinguishes the human is the ability to create images in one's mind. Clearly, whoever used this cave to hone his or her visions was not one of the first humans but rather a member of a culture that had already developed complex forms of religion, social life, and economy. Still, I can imagine, alone in the ancient bowels of rock and shadow, that whatever image might be created to account for its invisible presence would take the form of the godlike, the nonhuman, or perhaps some blend of both.

Four figures are painted at the left of the entrance, clustered together and surprisingly small, given the monstrous size of the cave: two one-armed anthropomorphs, one with a shield; one a turtle-shape, or *therianthropomorph*, part human and part animal in form; and what looks like a human riding an animal or an animal with a long neck or headdress, or, on closer inspection, a bison or elk stabbed with two spears. Together, they occupy about two square feet in a vault at least thirty feet in height. One of the anthropomorphs is so faded that I didn't see it at first. It floats like an apparition, neither on the rock or in it. The French philosopher Maurice Merleau-Ponty speaks of experiencing the same phenomenon when faced with the images on the cave walls of Lascaux: "The animals painted on the walls of Lascaux are not there in the same way as are the fissures and limestone formations. Nor are they *elsewhere*. Pushed forward here, held back there, supported by the wall's mass they use so adroitly, they radiate about the wall without ever breaking their elusive moorings. I would be hard pressed to say *where* the painting is I am looking at."[43]

The theory, widely accepted now by most archeologists and confirmed by oral records from many American Indian tribes, that rock art is a product of shamanic or shamanistic behavior, was not always the prevailing one. Since the discovery of Altamira in Spain and Lascaux in France, ideas as to the purpose of rock art have ranged widely and have, at various times, been used to interpret pictographs and petroglyphs in the Americas. According to Lewis-Williams, who summarizes these theories in his book *The Mind in the Cave*, archeologists first believed the figures to be a product of early peoples' need to decorate their surroundings, a desire for beauty inherent in the human brain, or they believed the paintings were products of hunting magic, the figures drawn to increase fertility of prey or to literally draw the animals closer, a willed visualization of what they wanted to find outside the door of the cave, or they believed the signs might be read as directional or notational, pointing to underground springs or trails over the pass. Until recently, the guides on a popular boat trip through the Gates of the Mountains on the

Missouri interpreted a rock shelter pictograph, visible from the water, as directing attention to a buffalo jump on the other side of the river. Most of these theories, however, have holes in them. (Why indeed would the very same people who used the buffalo jump have a need to direct themselves to it?) Although some rock art signals important places—the arrow in the preparation area, for instance, pointing to the initiation site at Hellgate Gulch—most are found in places that are clearly a destination in themselves. Often, too, animals depicted are not animals a people would have relied on for food—elk or reindeer are rarely depicted, for instance, in the European caves—and how do we explain the hundreds of half-animal, half-human, half-god figures or the geometric abstractions?

"There is more to the mind than just intelligence: there is also consciousness,"[44] Lewis-Williams writes, and believes this helps to explain not only the images found in caves at Lascaux and Chauvet, but in rock shelters in Montana and Australia, and those painted by Bushmen in South Africa, in effect, by the makers of rock art all over the world. Although it is, of course, dangerous to generalize across time and regions, race and gender, Lewis-Williams' theory is based on the fact that we share, as *Homo sapiens,* the same brain as those who were painting on the walls of caves 30,000 years ago. "There is no doubt in any researchers' minds that Upper Paleolithic people had full modern language,"[45] he writes, as well as the ability to remember, manipulate, and share mental imagery. Alexander Marshak concurs: "For us the important thing is the combined evidence for an evolved, modern, cognitive, and symbolic capacity found in the earliest levels to the last."[46]

What is most relevant to speculations as to the purpose of rock art is that this same brain is capable of experiencing what Lewis-Williams calls the "spectrum of consciousness," with ordinary wakeful awareness on one end of the spectrum and full trance, wherein the sensory world falls away and is replaced with visual and auditory hallucinations, on the other. All Homo sapiens are equipped to experience dreams, and, although those dreams might differ, the neurological processes that produce them do not. In the absence of sensory stimuli, or when the brain is starved for food, or as the body begins to sleep, or under the influence of mind-altering drugs such as peyote or tobacco, or in states of extreme illness such as fever, or in trance induced by rhythmic or repetitive sound or movement, the mind world-wide behaves in the same way, Lewis-Williams claims. During the first stage, such as the first slippage into sleep or that of a migraine headache coming on, a person "sees" what are variously called phosphenes or form constants or entoptic images.[47] These are images produced by the mind itself, created somewhere between the eye and the cortex of the brain, and consisting of zigzag lines, arcs, circles, series of dots, sunbursts, broken lines, etc., images that we find on almost any pictograph or petroglyph panel. Neurological studies have found that the human brain produces these images fairly consistently. They are, Williams argues, the images we see in Australian sand paintings, as well as the mysterious geometric patterns found at Lascaux.

As the mind goes deeper into trance, toward what Lewis-Williams calls "the intense autistic end of the spectrum," the brain tries to make sense out of what it sees (which is really the workings of the brain itself) and attributes the series of lines or dots to the back of a bison or the feathers of a bird. It is this stage that is culturally determined and the reason that images differ from France to America to Africa. One makes sense out of what one sees because of what one has seen before, whether in nature or on the walls of previously painted caves. The third stage is more mysterious. "As one moves into stage 3, where hallucinations take place, many people experience a swirling vortex or tunnel."[48] In some cultures, it is experienced as entering a hole in the ground. This is the stage where the dreamer steps into the vision, participating in what he or she is seeing: "Finally, in this stage, subjects enter into and participate in their own imagery: they are part of a strange realm."[49]

All people dream. Some people experience visions. Some cultures are built around certain individuals' ability to do so, yet all of us are capable of it. Our brains, as Lewis-Williams says, are "wired to experience the intensification of the trajectory in the spectrum of consciousness," a spectrum which includes "ordinary" rational consciousness and the ability of people to enter the earth or go flying through the sky. In between are thresholds where spirits exit and emerge, fringes of hematite mixed with deer blood, dreams and starbursts and anxious doodling. The cave fills with color and meaning. The dreamer squeezes through tunnels or is torn apart and sewn back up. He encounters helpers: possible shield-bearing figures, buffalo, spears. Acrobats. Theriomorphs. The Great Mother of the Animals. One can see that value does not have a stable place on this kind of spectrum, that madness and vision and ecstasy are thus, as Lewis-Williams writes, "culturally defined."[50] As well, one might say, as culturally navigated.

We can agree that there is no definite way of knowing what individual pictographs mean, especially those painted a thousand and more years ago, those with no ethnographic record associated with them. Even the so-called "tally marks" or finger smears, which appear at many sites in the western part of Montana, might count the number of days spent undertaking rituals or the number of rituals performed, or the number of spirit guides who appeared to the seeker.[51] We don't know if the images were painted right after or days after the initial vision was experienced. (Most experts concur that most of the figures were not painted in trance. The lines are too delicate, too assured.) The red handprints that appear at so many sites, hands either painted and pressed against the rock or held there while paint was blown or sprayed to form an outline, could mark the site where a vision came out of the rock or they might be the first step in the process of initiation. But, if we consider most pictographs as being made by people who have experienced "alternative" points on the trajectory of consciousness, whether in stage one where they begin to see entoptic images or in stage three when they are interacting with the spirit guides themselves, we might learn something about the imagination and the human mind.

I consider the study of rock art the study of the Imaginary Art of the Interior. The Underworld, one might say. The paintings and etchings are made by practitioners of the interior vision, shamans and vision questers. They are made by those people whom Jerome Rothenberg famously called, in his book of "the ritual-systems of which so much poetry is a part," *Technicians of the Sacred*.[52] The shaman, a skilled technician at coming in and out of these alternative states, goes into trance at specific sites because they are places proven to be conducive to penetration into the underworld, just as, in later times, the Romans entered the cave of the sibyl or visited the volcanic lake at Averno. As people begin to share those experiences— through images painted on walls or shields or chunks of bone, through the language of storytelling or metaphor—a previously invisible world begins to form. Lewis-Williams writes that "by such socializing of mental imagery, [homo sapiens are able to] conceive of an 'alternative reality,' a 'parallel state of being' or 'spirit world' so memorable and emotionally charged that it had a factuality and life of its own."[53]

The shaman enters the rocks to meet the spirit beings there,[54] rock wall as site both where spirit emerged out of rock and where image emerged out of brain. The Underworld. Hell. Hades. What exists there? One thinks of the most famous depiction of it in Dante's *Inferno*, a Christian construction mapped with particular sites designed for various punishments for different sins. The Hades of Homer's time was a cold, shady, undefined and distant place where apparitions, ghosts of what they used to be, wander restlessly, unreachable. Odysseus, the hero, venturing into this realm, can only go as far as the entrance to Hades where he pours libations of blood, which the dead flock to, in order to bring them to speech and thus, prophesy for him his way home. Psychoanalyst James Hillman, in his book *The Dream and the Underworld*, states, "'Entering the underworld' refers to a transition from the material to the psychical point of view."[55] At the same time, this underworld, we know from accounts of Greek myth, Dante, and the stories of shamans, has a specific and particular, even sacred, geography of its own and is inhabited not only by the dead but by powerful spirits. Eschleman, who spent over thirty years studying and writing about the Ice Age cave art of France, writes that it is possible to look at cave paintings as representations of this geography, that "cave images painted or engraved 25,000 years ago, via dreaming and imagining, [might have] transformed cave 'insides' into an underworld construction."[56]

Certainly the act of entering a cave, whether the deep and winding tunnels of French caves or the large open shelters of Montana, and whether one had to crawl on one's hands and knees through narrow openings or one sat in the folds of a cliff for days and nights open to stars and sky, replicated a journey into the deep recesses of earth. "Entry into Upper Paleolithic caves," Lewis-Williams writes, "was probably seen as virtually indistinguishable from entry into the mental vortex that leads to the experiences and hallucinations of deep trance."[57] In fact, it seems conducive to it. One can imagine, in a place such as the cave by Lion's Head, presences watching from the upper ledges, snouts and shoulders and antlers emerging out of the wildly sinuous and bulbous forms of the rock. Even more so, one imagines, if there were a fire flickering, a tallow lamp, which would start them moving. Who are we to say whether the figures and guides encountered are inside the cave of the mind or produced by the mind of the cave itself?

"Worldwide, shamans describe their initial trance experiences as involving flight, levitation, or stretching or foreshortening limbs and bodies to enter the spirit world through cracks or holes (often in cliffs or rocks)," write Keyser and Klassen.[58] And once they are there, what do they encounter? In America, the boat-shaped deer, bison, turtle, prairie chicken, bear, snake, thunderbird, and lizards. In Europe, aurochs (ancient oxen), bison, bear, rhinoceros, wild horses, and birds. In Africa, the elands (ancient antelopes). Sometimes there are human-like figures in relation to these things; however, they are often *anthropomorphic* with antlers, wings, or no arms, or they are their*anthropomorphic*. There is never an indication of landscape in rendering these murals of the underground world—mountains or rivers or roads—though some of the so-called "weapons" might as soon be specific plants, ferns or blades of grass, and the artists sometimes take advantage of a horizon line formed in the rock—think of the famous "swimming stags" of Lascaux. The question that intrigues me though is this: Why are so many animals populating the underworld? Why is it that animals are there to meet whomever has the courage to cross into it?

"There is an imagination below the earth that abounds in animal forms, that revels and makes music," writes Hillman.[59] Hillman's remark seems to refer to the Dionysian; however, I am thinking of something much earlier, perhaps even original to it. The Upper Paleolithic dates range from 35,000 to 9,000 B.P., the time when figures of animals began to appear on cave walls in southern France and Spain. Spreading out from Africa 90,000 years ago or more, the early Homo sapiens who made them traveled north to the Dordonge area, then further into Siberia, some of them crossing the Bering Strait, and entering North America 12,000 to 20,000 years ago. North American peoples—whether their descendents or people aboriginal to the North American continent itself—drew animals on the rocks. Lewis-Williams tells of a tribe in California called the Yokuts whose shamans believed that it was the animals that "opened" the rock shelter walls to the underworld for them. Quoting from an interview with a Yokuts man in the 1930s, he writes that once inside, it was the animals that told him what to do.[60]

Why animals? Eschleman, in his book *Juniper Fuse*, speculates that the Upper Paleolithic was a time when humanity was distinguishing itself from all other species and that rock art was a projection of that distinction. It is difficult for us to imagine a time when human beings weren't peripheral to the great herds, yet this major evolution, if we follow archeologists such as Lewis-Williams, from Neanderthal brain to that of the Homo sapiens, made it possible to actually *see or imagine* oneself and thus to compare oneself with other species. As Eschleman writes, "the liberation of what might be called autonomous imagination came from within as a projective response on the part of those struggling to differentiate themselves from, while being deeply bonded to, the animal."[61]

In Eschleman's theory, the origins of image-making (and by extension, the origin of art) come from the human need to separate from the herd, that by making an image outside of oneself, one has control over what one projects. If one is the artist, one is no longer animal. The animal has become *other*. That would explain why we so seldom see people in the art of the Paleolithic, just as when we dream, we rarely see ourselves, our physical body projected in the dream. Eschleman speculates that it is our knowledge of the difference between us and animals that we project on the cave wall. People painted the figures of animals on the walls of caves because they could, by doing so, imaginatively and religiously, separate themselves from other species, in order better to see themselves and their role in a new world.

This "liberation of what might be called autonomous imagination" would not have come without cost. The expulsion of the *animal that we are* in order to define ourselves as the *human that we are*, a forceful expression of self-differentiation and self-estrangement, as Eschleman frames it, must have caused a great deal of ambivalence and tension. What might consciousness have been like, suddenly awake to the difference between animal and human, and yet confused by that separation, no longer dependent on the great herds but lord over them? Eshleman writes, "I began to see prehistoric psychic activity as a swamplike churning in which creative and destructive forces were entwined in such a way that a person seeking to know them could hardly tell them apart. To enter the prehistoric cave of one's own mind then . . . would be to enter a realm of darkness under the rule of possibly a single massive core. I envisioned this core as amoebic, as an energy flow and restricting membrane that had been activated by the much earlier catastrophic separation between animal and hominid."[62]

Eshleman's theory, however, does not explain the visionary nature of the cave paintings. It ignores the fact that contemporary shamans have stated that they go into their trances *in order to connect*, not separate from, the animal spirits, and that this connection—and the resulting pictographs—were seen to benefit the entire community. Why would initiates return again and again to these sites, if they already knew they were different from the animals? What shamans and initiates seek, instead, when they encounter these sacred places is not difference but recognition: the power of origins. Though our evolved brain gave us incredible advantage over other animals, with its increased capacity for memory, for communication, for image-making and sharing, so that we could tell time, anticipate the migrations of our food sources, plan for pregnancy and weather, there was also something that was lost.

An ancient tie, perhaps. Even twenty thousand years later, we can identify the same longing to reconnect with nature, and with an earlier past. Every culture has a story of being able to communicate with birds, animals, plants, even rocks. We see it in the rituals of North American tribes, the Deer Dance, the Prairie Chicken Dance, wherein the dancers turn into those whom they are depicting. We see it in Bernini's Daphne turning into a tree. We encounter it in the philosophy of romanticism as late as 1800. The German romantic poet Novalis writes, "I've heard it said that in the olden days, animals, rocks, and flowers all spoke to humans. I'm haunted by the idea that they have something to tell me, and I feel as if I could comprehend their speech."[63] In fact, the belief that we can communicate with the many forms of non-human life seems fundamental to any conception of the visionary, as well as the theology of those who made the pictographs and petroglyphs. One wonders if the very origins of metaphor indeed might be in the human imagination watching itself turn from animal into human, and then choosing to reverse this transformation, turning back into animal, which is exactly what the shaman does. Perhaps these transformations—which are both real and figurative at the same time—might be re-enacting this "catastrophic separation" and, in doing so, attempting to repair this ancient rift.

Do our deepest memories as animals lie literally inside the earth? Does the underworld consist of what we have left behind? (One thinks, too, of all the animals that our presence has relegated to the underworld by extinction.) Yet, if they are still accessible, albeit only by those initiated into the mysteries of entering earth, into a belief in the on-going nature of those animals, our need to be close to them, not separate from them, must be part of this way of knowing. Further, could it be that Paleolithic people conceived of the immortal part of animal or humankind that continues its existence after death, a concept for which there is no other word but soul, because of their travels in trance to this deeper world? Although historians of religion such as Erwin Rohde have placed the beginning of the philosophy of the soul with the Greeks, even he speculates that the Dionysian rites that led up to it were of much more ancient origin.[64] Could it be that before Greece, before Thrace, before the tribes-people who came down to the cities with their rites of ecstatic trance and interchange with spirits, belief in the soul was handed down for tens of thousands of years? And is the soul animal?

❋

According to Mircea Eliade in his classic book *Shamanism: Archaic Techniques of Ecstasy*, shamanism originated in Siberia and Central Asia, though it can be found on every continent, and can be defined as "one of the archaic techniques of ecstasy."[65] It can thus be defined as an experience occurring at one of Lewis-Williams' alternative ends of the spectrum of consciousness. Documented by the earliest travelers in Central and North Asia, it is a technique wherein, by means of drums, chants, and fasting, the shaman goes into a trance where he is able to, as Eliade says of a Tungas shaman, "understand the language of nature."[66] Although each shaman has her own "cache" of tutelary animals and spirits, songs and prayers and signs, there are similarities in experience for those who have braved the spirit world: ritual dismemberment in the initiation process, removal of organs, descent under the earth, and then magical ascent to the sky, where they are given prophetic and healing powers.[67] Some shamans mentioned climbing to the sky on a tree, some on a rope, some on a spiral staircase, and some would simply fly. On their way, they would meet their helpers, birds or animals, the spirits of deceased shamans, gods, and divine beings, who directed them and gave them powers.

The language that these helpers speak is discernable only to the shaman. Although, as Lewis-Williams writes, "In shamanistic belief, images and visions are not silent: they speak, make animal sounds and communicate,"[68] those animal sounds are not the sounds animals make in the real world. The language is one only encountered in the visionary or dream world, a secret shamanic language with which spirit helper and shaman are able to traverse the divide between them. "Animal language," Eliade writes, "is only a variant of 'spirit language.'"[69] In some visions, the shaman encounters only the presence of an animal; in some, they speak. In some, he or she rides on its back or otherwise enlists its aid in his or her journey. At other times, the shaman actually becomes the animal. In fact, it is an old shamanic practice, as it is an imaginative one, to concentrate on the body of an animal or tree or mountain, until one becomes that tree or mountain. This does not mean, Eliade warns, that the shaman is possessed by the figure; rather, the shaman "turns himself" into that figure. It is a measure of his power that he can do so. Whereas Eschleman speculates that cave art expresses humankind's withdrawal from the animal, Eliade writes that "Each time a shaman succeeds in sharing in the animal mode of being, he in a manner re-establishes the situation that existed *in illo tempore*, in mythical times, when the divorce between man and the animal world had not yet occurred."[70]

The origin of the word *verse* is the Latin *versus*, meaning to turn, to plow or transform line by line, and it is possible to imagine this kind of prosodic metamorphosis as distant analogue of the shaman's metamorphosis of being, enacted to speak to the ancient powers in an attempt to heal, to prophesize, to control the weather, and to meet with invisible forces. Robert Calasso, in his book *Literature and the Gods*, speculates that the sound of poetry itself was taken from the "feet" of the animals, that part of its transformative power is in its mimesis of the goat step or deer step in their dance: "The meters are sacred power; the skin of the black antelope is the form of sacred power; he puts on shoes of antelope skin; not to be hurt, he wraps himself in meters before approaching the fire." [71] This metamorphosing shares with the later arts its emphasis on the active use of what has been called the creative imagination. Key to the power of this imagination, Harrison writes, is that, unlike in dreams, in visions one "*sees* himself enter 'into another body, another character.'"[72] Creative imagination distinguishes itself from the simply imaginary by its active nature. Again, the shaman, or the poet or artist, is not passive, is not possessed: "Novices learn to do this," Lewis-Williams writes, "by 'actively engaging and manipulating the visionary phenomena.' Allied to this engagement is 'guided imagination,' a form of imagination that goes beyond what we normally understand by the word: in [anthropologist Leena] Siikala's phrase, it consists in 'setting aside the critical faculty and allowing emotions, fantasies and images to surface into awareness.'"[73] One becomes a character in the story of the transformation itself.

The shaman's act of entering the earth and meeting with and literally becoming the animals and spirits of our origins, in order to reunite with those powers, could be the very beginning of all image-making, of the pictographs and petroglyphs on cave walls in Paleolithic Europe and North America, of the early Dionsyian rituals wherein the dancers become the animals whose antlers and hides they wore, of the myths of men turning into gods turning into beasts and back again written down in Ovid's *Metamorphosis*. Perhaps the origin of metaphor *is* shamanic ritual, the imagination at its apogee, a speculation that has inspired many of the writers I have been quoting in this essay, as well as others. Harrison, speaking of Nietzche's *Thus Spake Zarathustra*, writes that Nietzsche, in contemplating how to heal that ancient rift between the human and the animal, "envisions an evolutionary miracle of the will" in which human beings can bridge that gap, coming "full circle back to the earth and its species, bridging the chasm that separates humanity from the animal kingdom. The bridging is a metamorphosis, and it goes by the name of Dionysos, who is at once beast and god."[74] Or perhaps Dionysos is a late-comer in the chain.

I think of the men here in Montana who are ecstatic at the thought of gaining a wolf tag now that they have been de-listed from federal protection. I think of the mule deer, or what was left of it, piled neatly alongside my road this winter, how the hunter had built a pile of its legs and balanced its head on top so that it stared out at whomever walked by, its eyes gouged out by the ravens. I think of my neighbor's horror show of a living room, crammed with the mounted heads and tanned skins of over thirty species, including musk ox, bison, ermine, caribou. Tribute or joke? Private perversion or truncated ceremonial? The animals were here when we, as Homo sapiens, arrived, when we awakened. They are the old ones, the ancient ones, ancestors we do not acknowledge in waking life. Great Mother of the Animals, the shamans called one of the spirits they visited under the earth. We love them, dream about them, write about them, paint them— our imaginations as well as our bodies feed off them—and yet we also destroy them, as well as their habitats.

The history of shamans and shamanic societies does not speak well for their ability to persevere against the forces of modernity. The Soviets executed or imprisoned the shamans of the Eveky or Eveny tribes, thus confusing and scattering their leadership. There are stories of Soviet pilots dropping suspected shamans from planes over the steppes, taunting them to try to fly.[75] In the 1920s and 1930s, shamans, head tribesmen, or anyone who had influence over the old ways were hunted down and destroyed or made the object of disrespect: "With their trances and soul-flights, shamans were an irritating challenge to Communist missionaries of rational science who denied any other understanding of the world apart from their own. Whereas native people regarded shamans as channels to an ultimate reality made manifest through the actions of spirits, Soviet doctrine downgraded them to cynical, exploitative conjurers, or psychologically deranged individuals. Conspicuous by their elaborate robes and the sound of drumming far into the night, shamans were picked off one by one."[76] The history of Native American tribes after white contact is a well-documented trail of attempted genocide, with forbidden language, music, and ceremonies in its wake. The Ghost Dance movement, which ended tragically at Wounded Knee in 1890, with the deaths of at least 153 Lakota Sioux men, women, and children, is only one of the more notorious.

Yet like the reindeer, the shaman persists in the imagination of all people, an imagination evolved from long ago, when god wasn't human but perhaps musk ox or bear, a time when we shared a living, symbolic, and spiritual relationship with the animals. "In a general way," Eliade writes, "it can be said that shamanism defends life, health, fertility, the world of 'light,' against death, diseases, sterility, disaster, and the world of 'darkness.'"[77] The war-like implements that can be seen in many Paleolithic pictographs—spears, shields, bows, etc.—are not only for hunting animals but in defense against demons who might hurt the community. It was dangerous business to be a shaman; it was dangerous business to enter into those realms without one's helpers or guides. As it is dangerous now, it seems, to enter a world of disease, war, torture, and rape without them. "The shaman's essential role in the defense of the psychic integrity of the community," Eliade writes, "depends above all on this: men are sure that *one of them* is able to help them in the critical circumstances produced by the inhabitants of the invisible world."[78]

A friend tells me that, as a child in Anaconda, Montana, she participated in an initiation rite with other neighborhood boys and girls wherein they had to crawl through a natural tunnel in rock, a tunnel so dark they could not see a hand held in front of their faces. She said there was not enough room to turn around, nor could they at first see the opening at the other end. Everyone *had* to do it, or they were teased mercilessly for being afraid. One wonders at the courage of shamans crawling deep into caves, squeezing or swimming through narrow openings with no light but that from a small tallow lamp. Or the courage of the lone vision quester awake for days without food or water, waiting for some spirit from another world to begin its approach on a starless night. What if, while in trance, she tried to crawl out, became disoriented and crawled the wrong way, further in? Did people ever die in the caves? Did grizzly bears or cougars or wolves circle the rock shelter where the young boy was praying? Coming to an initiation site, or embarking on one's search for vision was, of course, an experience conducted under a wholly different consciousness. It took place within a culture that celebrated vision, had faith in a communion with the earth and its spirits, had rituals and trained professionals who presided over every step of the way. One did not brave the dark and the underground without preparation like the children of Anaconda, who experienced only fear, not vision, only thrill, not spiritual renewal.

I recently heard a news program about China on the radio that focused on how the country people are flocking to the cities for work in the factories, and abandoning the ancient villages. Suddenly, almost overnight, a boy who was scrawny and active, who knew the calls of birds, knew the wild plants and the haunts of animals, has access to a hundred television channels. Here in America, we have had generations to accustom ourselves to this change. And it is a different interior we have become used to, one devoid of bird-spirits and vision. If, as Lewis-Williams says, the brain is "hard-wired" to dream and vision and ecstatic state, what happens when the spectrum of consciousness shrinks? The visions that gave people courage for the buffalo jump and the hunt, for the wars that were fought, the winters suffered, that gave them endurance in childbirth and guidance into old age, into the days ahead, the visions that let them know they were not alone on the earth, that they could count on its many helpers and friends—what will we become without them?

❋

When we exit the cave at Lion's Head, the canyon is calling out with its colors and signs: animals, antlers, starbursts. The bells are ringing. The path is resonant. We see so many figures on our way down the trail that we talk of coming back the next day with a camera, but the light, we know, will be different and we might see nothing. Illusions? No, it is that sometimes things shine forth: shadows of leaf and stem and spider web and hand against rock and ground. The sun enters the forest as a kind of wind, sweeping the ceiling of leaves, waking the figures, then, as easily, it is gone. The young boys on motorcycles practicing on the hillside until there is no vegetation left wave to us as we walk to the car. A marmot is dead on the road we came in on—someone had to aim for it, we say to each other, accelerate on this slow, winding gravel road to hit it. Brown trees on the slopes. Beetles, they say, following a swath, a path to the north, though all trees are susceptible because of the heat and the drought. Overwhelming, what needs to be healed.

I learn later that this particular cave, of which I was so frightened, is one of the most visited pictograph sites in Montana, that hundreds of teenagers hike to it each week in the summer, due to the two church camps situated below. Inside, they eat lunch, take photos, fool around. Near Kalispell, cars speed by on Highway 2 past the Falling Buffalo pictographs, having no clue what is just outside their side windows. Driving eighty miles an hour to Missoula on the interstate, one can glimpse the strange orange-red of ochre off the cliffs to the right if one knows where to look, though most people, even most people from Montana, drive by and have never seen them. Sometimes I think that our culture's ignorance and neglect of rock art is good, that it is an invisible shield that protects many of these sites from vandalism and destruction. Still, if I take the frontage road exit, park my car in the gravel beside the road, and make my way up to the pictographs—a high circle within a circle, two anthropomorphs with arms raised, countless finger smears— even in winter I am following the tracks of others pressed into the snow. Sometimes I find tobacco left on a ledge, sometimes a partial braid of sweetgrass. The bushes next to a site just off the Flathead River are tied with cloth pouches, strips of fabric, cigarettes, and other gifts. Wherever I have encountered pictographs or petroglyphs, there is always sign that people still visit, not perhaps in large groups of initiates led by medicine men or those who stay for days seeking a vision, but briefly, quietly, and with purpose.

IV

*There are only a handful of primary incidents in life, incidents powerful enough to create cracks or boundary lines that we'll often enter and follow for years before another crucial event pounds us deeper or reorients us to a new map. As we approach these events omens appear everywhere, the world becomes dangerously magical, as if we had called the gods, and the gods were now answering.*

—Clayton Eschleman[79]

Six years ago, I drove two days through the wintry and wind-swept plains of eastern Montana and Wyoming to my position as Visiting Writer at the University of Wyoming in Laramie. Always on the lookout for birds, I was pleased when, at first, I passed three or four bald eagles perched in the bare cottonwoods along the coulees. Soon, I was counting twenty, thirty, a hundred, and I realized that I was amidst a January eagle migration. Since there are few trees in this area of the country, the eagles—both bald and golden—stood on boulders in the fields or grouped together atop haystacks. At the time, not knowing that my life would change drastically by the time I returned, I was charmed by the envoy accompanying me. I felt they were blessing me as I made my way to a new job. Once I arrived, however, I became immersed in my teaching and writing, the meeting of new colleagues and students, and I forgot about the eagles. It was in Laramie, though, that the animal dreams began: fawns trying to crowd into the back of my car, a marmot curled up on the driver's side, a raven braiding my hair, hopping from one side to the other picking up strands in its beak and looping them, armadillos, kittens, a lid I pried open to reveal a barrelful of songbirds. The dreams were not a zoo; the animals weren't caged. One night I dreamt of a tree infested with black flies and hundreds of blackbirds that came to eat them. A week later, the town was full of them, their clown cries, loud and social, so that I began thinking of my dreams as a place, in this case, a stopping place on their migration, but in other cases, a manger, a stable, a gathering hole for these strange figures who came visiting.

Though the animals had a feel of death to them, not the sad or grotesque features of death but the luminous part, the transformative, I did not try to interpret them. There were too many of them, they came too frequently, and it seemed beside the point, as if their arrival alone was a secret, catastrophic language, a language, strangely, that had no meaning, per se, but was an end in itself. In fact, it seemed to eschew meaning. The contemporary Syrian poet Adonis, writing about the poetic language of Sufism and religious *shari'a* language, differentiates between what he calls a language of love and a language of explanation: "The former loves things without necessarily understanding them, while the relationship of [the latter] to things and the universe is one of understanding, knowing and valuation rather than love. Love itself is not expressed but experienced. You can convey images of it, but, in essence, it is like the absolute, impossible to talk about, because it is beyond the borders of logic and reason. In other words, it is beyond speech."[80] The animals in my dreams did not speak, as animals, birds, and trees in the wild do not. They gestured clumsily or with grace; they pooled and spread out into the corners. One way to say it would be that their images took on a life of their own. (Another way, as I have previously mentioned, is Corbin's description of the image as an "organ of perception," a way of knowledge that functions beyond or before thought.)

One week before the end of the semester, I received a call from my partner, whom I had been with for over twenty-three years, telling me that she was leaving me for someone else, that, in fact, she had already moved out. The future of my summer, my home, my identity, my life was to change drastically and irreparably from what I had expected, and I was thrown without warning deeply into grief. In retrospect, it seems as if the animals were less a warning than an accompaniment, less a prophesy than a symptom of the cracking of the foundation to come. In Laramie, before the break, which separated my life into the before and the now, which occurred not only in the mundane life of the emotional and narrative, but in what I would like to call soul time, I felt the signs amassing. I was shattered. And it was at that crucial juncture, when most of the ties to my known life were severed, directionless, bewildered, that I was invited to float the Smith River with friends, encountering the pictographs, in Indian Cave, for the first time.

Was there an essential difference between the eagles accompanying me on the road through Wyoming and the blackbirds that infiltrated my dreams there? "Unfortunately in English," Hillman writes, "we have but one word, 'image,' for after-images, for perceptual images, dream images, illusory images, and for imaginative metaphorical ideas."[81] Sensory perception. Thoughts. Memory. Trance. Vision. Metaphor. Symbol. Or alternately: Pictograph. Petroglyph. "Male Dancer Transforming into Deer Shape." Spirit Guide. Poem. The spectrum of consciousness, like the spectrum of light, is a way to describe the miracle of seeing. As light can be divided into a series of colored bands dispersed and arranged according to their wavelengths, so, too, the images we encounter range widely. Any one of them could be a door. Those who made the pictographs painted their mental vision on the wall, but when they left they carried that vision with them. It was their power, their medicine. Those who visit the pictographs, whether to scrape paint off them, add their own handprints or finger smears, or simply look, carry those images off with them, too, albeit perhaps in a different form. They might write them. They might paint or dream them.

Whether the image is a pictograph of a falling buffalo, a dream of deer walking through snow, or real chickadees landing on my real shoulders at the feeder, my study of rock art has set me exploring possible methods to more deeply engage with it, to move into it, live with it, as if, as Bachelard writes, one could use the image to learn to "think and dream at the same time," to live more widely along the spectrum. Again, I am not talking about interpreting or explaining, as in a Freudian or Jungian interpretation of dreams or an anthropologist's speculation as to the meaning of the pictographs. (To explain one loses sight of what one is seeing: "Thereby," Corbin writes, "the vision itself vanishes, its plastic aspect, corresponding to the soul's most secret anticipations, is destroyed."[82]) I am talking about an intensified relationship with what is seen, as a way to attempt a healing of the ancient rift between the human and the rest of nature. We cannot—most of us—be shamans, of course. However, the shamanic practice that attempts to *see* into another, to imagine oneself becoming another, is perhaps not only a lost art but a lost and essential practice of compassion at a time when we are increasingly unbalanced and alienated from the earth. What does it mean to be alive on an earth millions of years old, a species come out of the animal, and yet intent on destroying all other animals, capable of dreams, vision, language, the imaginative conception of an underworld or over-world for over thirty thousand years? We do not know. "Essential for working with what is unknown is an attitude of unknowing. This leaves room for the phenomenon itself to speak," Hillman writes.[83]

The animals live in the same world we do, of deep night and dawn, traveling the waterways and following the ancient paths of the blood. We sit inside knowing *deep down* what we have lost. We also know deep down what is retrievable. Hawk in its dark phase, elk prints that form gray pockets in the snow—the images change as they surface and retreat, become dream, memory, spirit buried under rock, vision inside the body, emerging as ochre painted on cave walls, as personal medicine or as poem. Eliade, at the end of his book on shamanism, speculates that many images in literature might be indeed "of ecstatic origin," that shamanic trance, which utilizes the imagination to enter into an interior world in order to participate in, not simply observe, that world and its narratives, is the origin of poetry itself. The shaman, Eliade writes, begins by preparing his trance, drumming, calling on his helpers, speaking "a 'secret language' or the 'animal language,' imitating the cries of beasts and especially the songs of birds. He ends by obtaining a 'second state' that provides the impetus for linguistic creation and the rhythms of lyric poetry."[84]

Two years ago, on a cold December morning, my friend picked me up for a drive on my birthday to a destination that was to be a surprise. We traveled south down a highway with which we are both familiar, through a tiny Montana town, and to its outskirts. We pulled into a ranch where my friend got out, knocked on a door, and spoke to a man who was about our age. "See that gray house," he said, pointing. "See that outcropping behind it?" We looked toward the end of a long ridge of foothills, as he gave us a hand-drawn map. "It's still on our property. Nobody will bother you up there." After passing many corrals and barns and fenced fields, we parked where a jeep trail climbed straight up the flank of a mountain, and my friend finally told me what we were there for, that we were going to a pictograph cave, one known only by the ranchers who own the land. We made our way up over a scattering of quartz to the top where the wind was biting and fierce. No cave in sight. We picked our way between sagebrush and a splintery desert bush that grabbed at our down jackets, me holding my hat down, trashing my boots on the shale. Then, my friend had a feeling that it might be to the south, facing the river. And it was. The opening had been gated with steel bars to prevent earlier vandalism but someone had pried part of it out so we were able to crawl in. The cave faced a perfect curve of the river below, which was what we call open, not frozen.

When we asked the rancher if he'd visited the cave a lot when he was growing up, he said no, the last time was forty years ago when "they took a bunch of us kids up there on a fieldtrip. Weird idea, tramping with a bunch of grade school kids through rattlesnake country," he grumbled. The cave was big enough to stand in, for a hundred people to stand in, bone dry as the entire West is right now, rocks the color of dust, and smeared inside with orange ochre that, if wet, would shine. Small pictographs, a star as we enter on the right, the softest of reds, and then, on the far wall facing the entrance, a figure, possibly two, the shaman perhaps, and many more stars surrounding him. As our eyes adjust, we realize the stars are not stars but more anthropomorphs. "How old is that figure," we ask, as we always do, and "Why?"

There are few Indians left in the Whitehall Valley where we find the star paintings. The tribal people we see on our seven reservations and in our cities, modern people, more modern than anyone, having survived attempted genocide, near starvation, the loss of the buffalo, the theft of their language and customs and land, are far from here. But they have survived. At their celebrations, at the powwows, young boys with long hair, wearing beaded flowers and birds and ribbons, still dance, though at the break, they are busy with texting on their cell phones. The young women in clutches, shy, dignified, smooth-faced, beautiful, make eyes at us. They are proud and sparkling and make us proud, until we remember the high teen suicide rate on reservations and the percentage of children who will graduate and we think of how hard it is for an Indian kid to stay alive.

We no longer require of all our young a quest for individual vision. Few people, at least in America, we are told, spend any time outside, let alone any time outside alone. And the fate of the animals, who are disappearing each day at an alarming rate, is cause for despair. Artists and poets, whom we might think of as some of the last remnants of those who practice an active and creative imagination that did its part in controlling the weather, speaking to and for the animals, healing illness and mitigating death, are viewed as apart from the overall community, not playing an integral role. The door to the underworld seems to be closing. The image, that "poetry or prose of correspondences and hieroglyphics," which connects us to that world, which "intuits analogies not immediately visible,"[85] is one that fewer people are able to see, let alone read. Yet as Lewis-Williams writes, the reason so many peoples around the world believe in passing underground to a subterranean realm is because in altered states of consciousness, they have experienced just that. And, because of the make-up of the human brain, we will continue to do so. We are all the descendents, whether directly or not, of those people who dreamed in the caves, rock shelters and along the bluffs, and who painted what they saw. Finlay, speaking about the aboriginal artists she met in Australia, writes that, despite the poverty and misery she found in some of the communities, "there was still a sense that below that ochre surface there is a different reality. It is a reality that the best red paint and perhaps the best art can give a glimpse of, but just a glimpse." One of the elder painters explained: "We don't know what it is, but something underneath, under the ground."[86]

L ate in his life, the painter Morris Graves, known for his symbolic and visionary renderings of animals, birds, and snakes, began to paint realistic portraits of flowers, which he arranged on his table or found at the street markets in Seattle. Hermetic, eccentric, having lived alone in the wilds of the Pacific Northwest, Graves was, as critic Theodore F. Morris writes, "famous for his commitment to the vision of 'the inner eye,'"[1] which had resulted in such metaphysical paintings as *Moon Chalice*, *Little Known Bird of the Inner Eye*, and *Millennium Light*. I remember the story of him listening in the night outside his island home and drawing—inventing!— animals for the sounds he heard. I remember his 'white writing,' which he adapted from the painter Mark Tobey, nests of lacy, squiggling lines encasing the *Bird Singing in the Moonlight*, or the discordant and troubling red and black pattern above the grasses in *Spring with Machine Age Noise#3*. Graves was a clairvoyant, someone able to see past the surface, with its colors and sounds, into the way light might affect the song of a bird or our industry affect the grasses. His images came from another realm, that of dream or focused meditation, rather than the objective world. For an artist "so profoundly convinced that art's primary purpose was to help advance spiritual consciousness," critic Theodore F. Wolff states, to paint a simple bouquet of flowers on his table was a dramatic departure. Why, at the end of his life, flowers?

In *Summer Twilight, Fruit and Flowers (Peruvian lily bouquets-yellow, two Borneo night-blooming flowers, and platter of apricots)*, it is the twilight I see first, a radiant aura around the yellow bouquets, the edges of the apricots on their celadon plate, a yellow powdered on the table top under the vases, not so much a reflection— the table is soft, not glossed—as an absorption of pollen. The vases, too, are soft, blue and green and clear and multi-cast with flower-light. The background and foreground are translucent, dappled with changing color as if they were windows hung with rice paper. And then, there are the flowers themselves, hieroglyphic and dreamlike in their reality, arrow-leafed, scalloped, more insect than any body akin to us, shaped like trumpets and dragonflies or something tangled and ancient found at the bottom of the sea.

Though the flowers are recognizably flowers, the table a table, a vase a vase, the paintings somehow highlight the strangeness that is the aliveness of plants, that sense, when we look closely at leaves or flowers or stems that, though they can't be anthropomorphized, though their shapes and colors don't belong to us, each one seems startlingly conscious, an individual, a person. As if each flower had developed its colors as one does a self. As if each flower had a secret name. What is astonishing, and what the painting makes us aware of, is that they are here, living in their completely alien, though parallel realm, right next to us. As poet John Yau states in the preface to *Morris Graves: Flower Paintings*, "In this century, one which has seen the rise of both abstraction and mechanical reproduction, Graves does something wholly unexpected and ultimately profound: he uses paint to restore to flowers their specific identity. He does so by halting at the edge of both abstraction and exactitude, by concluding at the limits of sight . . ." [2]

A curious notion: *the edge of both abstraction and exactitude.* Can it be regarded as the same edge? In my study of Graves' paintings, I have been made aware of many other painters who turned to flowers at critical junctures in their lives, painters who were often known for their modernist and post-modernist experiments with materials and form. The Impressionist painter Edouard Manet, in the last months of his life, weak and bed-ridden with syphilis, painted sixteen small and remarkable canvases depicting the bouquets friends brought to cheer him in his illness. "The vigor of each flower is contained in a kind of gesture, the gesture of the form of the flower, as distinctive as a name, and the light they return to us is as particular to their form and color as the sense of likeness we experience in front of one of the pastels of his friends," [3] writes Andrew Jorge in his introduction to a monograph of these paintings. Piet Mondrian painted flowers before his signature experiments in abstraction, and then he returned to them again and again, creating his highly abstract modernist grids in primary colors alongside his shaggy, shopworn chrysanthemums and top-heavy stalks of red amaryllis with blue stems. The "relationship between natural lyricism and geometrical abstraction" [4]—a phrase used by critic David Shapiro in speaking of Mondrian—seems to be less oppositional than creative, the flower, in particular, offering an image that moves between both, movement we see in the work of many other modern painters, including Odilon Redon, who didn't begin his floating bouquets until he was in his sixties, Georgia

O'Keefe, whose larger than life flowers appeared well after her experiments in abstraction, even Pop artist Andy Warhol who silkscreened unnamed flowers, as well as soup cans and Coke bottles. We have been educated to regard the abstract and representational, the symbolic and real, as antithetical. Yet photographers, such as Edward Steichen, Edward Weston, and Robert Mapplethorpe, while at the same time giving us strikingly edgy and un-sentimentalized images of war, machinery, and sex, have also given us some of the most moving, intimate, and, revelatory images of flowers. What drew these experimental artists to depict *Dying Sunflowers*, chrysanthemums, amaryllis, and *Heavy Roses*, which are certainly traditional, even stereotypic emblems?

Shape and color, of course, have always been attractive to painters, and flowers, most of us would agree, are attractive in shape and color. Every culture, it seems, enhances its surroundings by decorating with real or imagined flowers, from the beading on Ojibwa moccasins to the patterns on vessels from Africa or the rugs woven in Turkey. The archeologist Andrew Marshak believes that many of the abstract symbols on Paleolithic cave walls are not abstract at all but leaves and flowers of specific plants.[5] Shape, color, fragrance, even the names of flowers set us dreaming—*rose, hyacinth, lavender, violet, iris*—as if by merely saying them we could move from the ordinary to the extraordinary:

> I will have the gardeners come to me and recite
> many flowers, and in the small clay pots
> of their melodious names I will bring back
> some remnant of the hundred fragrances.

> —*Rainer Maria Rilke*[6]

In the catalog of a 2004 show entitled *The Flower as Image*, at the Louisiana Museum of Modern Art in Humleback, Denmark, a show in which many of the aforementioned painters and photographers appear, the curators write that "many modern artists go on painting flowers even though the subject is quite at odds with the self-understanding of modern art as a critical, innovative thing."[7] Flowers, unlike other subject matter such as fashion, architecture, or technology, do not change. But our conception of what is beautiful, as Charles Baudelaire famously said, is made up of the "fugitive, the contingent," as well as the "unchanging and the immutable."[8] Is there a specific challenge in painting flowers, then, besides the challenge of confronting beauty in a different—one might even say an uglier— historical time? (*How with this rage shall beauty hold a plea, whose action is no stronger than a flower?* Shakespeare asked.) Is it that flowers, because they are emblems of beauty across time and culture, confront artists with the ever-present formal challenge to, as Ezra Pound said, *make it new?* Or is it that true beauty, in itself, is a destroyer of emblems? "This transitory, fugitive element," Baudelaire writes, "*whose metamorphoses are so rapid*, must on no account be despised or dispensed with. By neglecting it, you cannot fail to tumble into the abyss of an abstract and indeterminate beauty,"[9] one that has lost its power to change the way we see.

Unless we are talking of landscape paintings such as Van Gogh's fields of sunflowers or poppies, flowers usually belong to the genre we call *still lives*, an oxymoron that many critics have pointed out. (It is said that American Indians could ambush and conquer regiments of white soldiers by simply sitting in tall grass and waiting for them to come to them. They could do so because we expect life to *move*.) Fruits and vegetables are arranged artificially on a table, sometimes a jug of wine or flask of olive oil, less frequently an animal, a fish or hare. The task of the still life painting is to bring to life that which is still. In Graves' case, what is stunning about the flowers is that, though they are *not us*, there is something about them that we recognize *in us*. What is that? Perhaps it is their stillness, their solitude. Perhaps it is their radiance. Perhaps it is the fact that they do not open up to us, and yet seem as if they could, a metaphysical challenge par excellence. "The paint becomes coldly voluptuous," Yau writes about the Graves' paintings, "and, in that regard, resembles the flowers themselves: sensual inhabitants of their own private domain," a phrase which echoes lines in a poem by Jules Supervielle, wherein he describes not flowers but people as "sensitive inhabitants of the forests of ourselves." [10]

It seems obvious that Graves did not quit seeing as a metaphysician when he began painting his winter and summer bouquets, just as Mondrian did not abandon his formal experiments when he painted his impossibly blue chrysanthemums. Their preoccupations, one could argue, were not with beauty so much as how to use visual form to express intangible and interior realities that were, of course, in dynamic relationship with the tensions created by a rapidly industrialized, and diminished, natural world. Flowers seem intrinsically to lend themselves to this effort as their forms and colors are timeless, cosmopolitan, and decidedly not human—neutral, in fact—and yet at the same time they mirror to us, albeit in a dramatically accelerated fashion, human processes, whether interior or exterior. They enter the world fragile. They bloom, decay, and die. They are ephemeral and yet joyously alive. They come to us concretely, already dressed in figurative language. As Yau writes, "Flowers are always both themselves and symbols to be read." [11]

The edge between abstraction and exactitude (representation) is a flickering edge where the symbol makes its home. "When I say: 'a flower!'" Stephané Mallarmé writes, "then from that forgetfulness to which my voice consigns all floral form, something different from the usual calyces arises, something all music, essence, and softness: the flower which is absent from all bouquets." [12] It is almost impossible to really see a flower, Mallarmé thought, clouded as it is by cliché, the "usual calyces." Writing in his 1803 essay, "Crisis in Poetry," he was speaking for a new and modern kind of symbol, one that did not attach the object as a referent to an already established religious or cultural system—the rose as symbol of the Passion of Christ, for instance. To release a flower from its representations might have been the same challenge to him as to these painters: "Why should we perform the miracle by which a natural object is almost made to disappear beneath the magic waving wand of the written word, if not to divorce that object from the direct and the palpable, and so conjure up its *essence* in all purity?" [13] The symbol, as we know, presumes an *other* that is deeply connected to it, a presence or essence underneath, or *beneath* what we know of it. For Mallarmé, the task was not to name it but to allow or conjure that essence.

Many of Graves' later flower paintings had their precursors in his earlier images meant to convey metaphysical realities, works such as *Vessel Seeking to Achieve Its Ideal Image Form*, *Chalice*, and *Joyous Young Pine*. These paintings "share the same, simple compositional device of two central formal elements—one, usually circular, above, and the other, usually vertical, directly underneath," Wolff points out. This "*one-over-one compositional formula*," [14] a circle over a line, an upside down exclamation mark, the astrological symbol for Venus and for woman, resembles, of course, a human head over a body, as well as a bloom over a stalk. Wolff suggests that it was, for Graves, a "visual metaphor for man's progressive spiritual evolution—from fragmentation and imperfection (the lower, earthbound forms) to wholeness and perfection (the moon/blossom)." [15] Shapiro says of Mondrian's individual stalks of chrysanthemum, sunflower, and amaryllis that "the thematic reduction to singleness [one flower] seems to speak often as a rhetorical devise: the flower for the body." [16] A phenomenology of the flower image might speak to this conundrum: the flower as the most real and the most abstract. The flower as body and the flower as soul.

## II

### The Flower as Body

> Tell me, is the rose naked
> or is that her only dress?
>
> *—Pablo Neruda[17]*

If one is an herbalist, or an amateur botanist, finding and identifying plants is often dependent on first encountering them during their time of flowering. As sprout or stem or grass blade or leaf, the plant fades into the general background green in the same way that we become *en masse* on the streets of our cities. To flower is to distinguish oneself by color, shape, and fragrance, to become as individualized as the face of the beloved.

Most of us can name our mother's or grandmother's favorite flower. My mother's is lilac; my grandmother's was gladiola. The idea that each kind of flower has a specific personality or quality or message to convey is the basis for a system of correspondences originating in Persia called *The Language of Flowers*, which reached the height of its popularity in Europe in the early 1900s, but which we still vaguely apperceive when we choose roses for our lovers or daisies or carnations for our friends. We find it in Stein's famous whispering of *eros* in "A rose is a rose is a rose is a rose," or in Blake's symbol of spoiled love, "The Sick Rose." (*O Rose, thou art sick! / The invisible worm / That flies in the night, / In the howling storm, / Has found out thy bed / Of crimson joy, / And his dark secret love / Does thy life destroy.*) [18] But allegory is not what makes the flower paintings of Graves or Mondrian or Manet distinctive. To allegorize is not to "restore to flowers their specific identity," as Yau wrote about Graves' paintings, but to blur those distinctions in favor of a meaning everyone can agree on. Allegory, writes Henry Corbin, in his book on the creative imagination *Alone with the Alone*, is but a degraded form of the Image, one in which we no longer see the individual flower in front of us. "Allegory is a rational operation, implying no transition to a new plane of being or to a new depth of consciousness." [19] The allegorical image stays where it was first nailed down, in Persia or in England in the early twentieth century. It quits speaking to us. The symbolic image, on the other hand, "announces a plane of consciousness distinct from rational evidence; it is the 'cipher' of a mystery." [20] What is the mystery contained in the image of a flower that we recognize in it something human, something flesh and blood and body?

We have been taught that one of the differences between animals and plants is that animals are able to move, yet science has shown us that plants, though rooted in one place, are highly mobile. Many plants, for instance, are heliotropic (*heliotrope* is the name for the sunflower), bending toward the sun. They send roots into the ground for nourishment and moisture—"the roots of a sunflower can reach down eight feet, nibbling, evaluating, growing toward the best sources of food," says Sharman Apt Russell in her book *Anatomy of a Rose* [21]—and sprout upward toward the light, a miraculous force counter to gravity which Goethe, a great plant enthusiast, named "levity." [22] Most plants turn, reach, open, close, and quiver with excitement, as we do. They flower and produce seeds. They suffer weather and time, age, and die back. Their abbreviated lives often serve, in poetry and paintings, as allegory, in accelerated fashion, of our own human life processes. Mondrian loved chrysanthemums, the unraveling, aging quality I love in the prairie paintbrush. Shapiro says Mondrian "revealed his sense of time and suffering" in these flowers. [23]

And then, there is sex. Except for the mosses, liverworts, conifers, cycads, ferns and gingko trees, all plants flower *in order to reproduce*, writes Russell. [24] Dressed flamboyantly and heavily perfumed, they attract the bees, butterflies, birds, and even mammals that will carry their pollen to the awaiting stigma of another flower. Wide open or seductive in their ploys of lip and tongue, they are shameless. Of Mondrian's flower paintings, so different than the rigid and programmatic grids of his modernist experiments, Shapiro observes, "They remained with their emotional curves a powerful force to trouble him." [25] Mondrian, celibate for the last part of his life, Graves, Mapplethorpe, and Warhol, who were gay, Manet suffering from syphilis—a psychosexual reading of these paintings will stall us as absolutely as an allegorical reading would, and is not the direction I would like to go in this essay. Yet the vulnerability of the flowers, their overt sexuality, their contrived attractiveness, to which we are always attracted, is most often described as female. "We might think of the flowers, then, as the real nudes in the oeuvre of Mondrian and place our embarrassment [that he is painting flowers rather than grids] as a fear of desire," writes Shapiro. [26]

None of us wants to subscribe to a polemic that assigns to objects or feelings a gender, and, in fact, "about eighty percent of flowers are hermaphrodites," containing both male and female sex organs. [27] Still, when I read the words of the German mystic poet Novalis—"Should plants perhaps be the products of the feminine nature and a masculine spirit," he asks. "And plants, say, the young girls—animals the *young boys* of nature?" [28]—I feel some truth in them beyond the obvious and stereotypic dualities of gentleness and brute force, beauty and the beast. When I was writing my second book of poetry, wherein each poem grew out of a concentrated meditation on an individual herb, weed, or flower growing in a circumference around my home in Montana, I thought I was compiling a personalized, albeit poetic, herbal. Like an herbal, many of the poems contained the history of the plants' origins and uses, as well as my own close observations. But as I wrote more and more of them, instead of my perhaps misguided intention to listen to the plant and hear what it might have to tell me of its life, they seemed rather to reveal a wisdom applicable to my own wounds—physical and emotional—as well as the spiritual and epistemological wounds of a larger world that has not only separated itself from nature but also from what I will call the feminine. In "Bluebell," I wrote:

> They are pebbles meant to fall,
> these petals
> death-bent, imperfect.
> Are all plants this *effeminate*?
>
> Like butterflies, the leaves
> cling to the stalk
> to dry their rain-pinched wings.
>
> If you have bells, then ring, heart
> of the overcast,
> bog-god of the bitter.
> I will learn to kneel to hear you.

The poems began to reflect a sensibility, even theology, particularly in accord with the concerns of women, with their emphasis on cycles of birth and death, illness and health, childhood and aging, in other words, to the processes of the body:

> Here, like a god in its particular uncurling, a bracken fan—brilliant—
>     dips its fin into the stream.
> There is the loud lap and snort of an animal trapped under ice.
> There is a woman's veil shrunk to a religion of brown.

or, in "Prairie Sage":

> A bouquet? A bride's bouquet
> of sage and all she knows. Subjugated,
> so we can search for her. Doubted, so we can

dream of her. As lackluster. Frenzied.
The blue lobes curled in. What then?

Mei-Mei Berssenbrugge, whose recent poems have also been an attempt to communicate with plants, animals, and insects, says of her method, in an interview with Lesley Scalapino, "In reality, it is difficult for me to tune into the thoughts of animals and insects. It takes time for me to become quiet and the animals are moving around. I could often receive 'instant messages,' but what I sent out myself tended to be pressured, and I don't think that is the best way for animals to take in meaning . . . A plant gives me more time to get to know it."[29] In her poem "Slow Down Now," she leads us through this process, moving from objective observation of herself and environment to a more and more subjective stance. We can literally watch the image of the plant being absorbed into her:

I've been sitting looking at this plant without feeling time at all, and my breathing is calm.

There are tiny white rosettes, and the whole bush is a glorious cloud of feathery pink seed-heads, here, in the arroyo.

Even with closed eyes, I see flowers in the center of my sight, new flowers opening out with pink petals illuminated by low sun behind me, and small gray green leaves.

There's no stopping this effusion.

Looking at the plant releases my mental boundaries, so time is not needed for experience.

Late afternoon is like a stage, a section of vaster landscape, and my mood is of a summer idyll.

The dry arroyo sparkles around us.

Meaning I come upon on wild land strikes me at first as a general impression, then joy suffuses me.

I accept that I've aged and that some friends have died.[30]

The last line arrives abruptly and yet not artificially. It has grown organically out of the images before. We can follow it back. Traditional beauty is what has initially caught the poet's attention, the "glorious cloud" that is the flower head gone to seed. It is dying back. But because she is in what Corbin would call "sympathy" with the plant, honing her attention, her breath calms, her body calms and she is suddenly not "feeling time at all." The flower has enabled a shift in consciousness. She is in plant time, so much so that she can see the plant with her eyes closed.

In the center of her sight—one wonders whether she means the center of her closed eye or being—an effusion, much like a blossom, is pouring forth. Is this unrestrained expression flowing from the plant or has it set something in motion inside her, a feeling that takes the image of the bud opening and then the incredible transformation into seed? "Compared with the leaf, the flower is a dying organ," writes J. Lehrs, quoted in *The Secret Life of Plants*. "This dying, however, is a kind we may aptly call a 'dying into being.' Life in its mere vegetative form is here seen withdrawing in order that a higher manifestation of the spirit may take place . . . In the human being it is responsible for the metamorphosis or organic process which occurs in the path from the metabolic to the nervous system, and which we came to recognize as the precondition for the appearance of consciousness within the organism."[31] Looking at the flower gone to seed, Berssenbrugge suddenly accepts her own aging and with it her grief for her friends, as if the flowering has made room for this acceptance. It is a new-found awareness she has *grown into*.

If there is an equivalent in human beings to flowering, perhaps it is in the way feeling overtakes us. I'm not sure what I mean by this, but when Berssenbrugge writes, in another poem, "There is an affinity between awareness and blossom,"[32] I read "awareness" not as a way of thinking but as a feeling, feeling not as an emotion but as a tool, a trans-sensory tool, that introduces us to a different way of perceiving. Flowers are capable of this kind of feeling; they surface and bloom. (Perhaps that is why they are so associated with the female, granted as women are with that permission.) Radiance flowers, as do ideas, love, and epiphanies in the body and in the mind. The flower as verb. Communication flowers, between people as well as between humans and plants, as in this last section from the aforementioned poem, "Slow Down Now":

One time, you may need a plant you don't yet know, in order to connect pieces in yourself or in a person you are trying to be with.

It may be a rosebush at the end of the road, a summer rose, whitish on the outside of each petal, and pink inside, expressing its gestalt visually.

When a plant receives this kind of communication, it begins altering the wavelengths its chemicals reflect in order to offer itself to your imaginal sight, for you to gather it.

The plant or another person will awake from embedding in the livingness of the world and take notice of your request.

The internal chemistry of plants is one primary language of response that they possess.[33]

The pairing of a plant with human feeling of loss, "in order to connect pieces in yourself or in a person you are trying to be with," whether that person is disconnected from you through death or distance or some other kind of estrangement, is an ancient pairing that Herbals are based on, the connection that we might call "healing" or making whole. One can encounter this pairing in hundreds of poems, as if in merely saying the name of a flower, its healing properties might be enacted. John Felstiner, in an essay about Paul Celan, published in *Parthenon West*, speaks of one form of the classical Romanian folk song called the *doîna*, wherein despair is paired with the name of a plant. In this folk song, which is sung while expressing real grief in tears, the first words are always *foaie verde*, literally "green leaf":

> Green leaf of the plantain,
> My heart is stacked with pain.
> Pale leaf of blue lilac,
> Mother does not come back.[34]

Like the old-fashioned Herbals, which seek to pair the virtues of a particular plant with an illness, in this form the singing of the plant name serves to provide consolation to the person who is suffering, as if the language itself awakened the spirit of the form it refers to. Felstiner calls it a "folk elegy." Here is Celan's version of it:

> With
> our pistil soul-bright,
> our stamen heaven-waste,
> our corona red
> from the purpleword we sang
> over, O over
> the thorn.[35]

As a boy in pre-occupation Romania, Felstiner writes, Celan kept a notebook wherein he recorded all the names of the flowers surrounding his village, until the hills and forests were barred to the Jews. "An acute awareness, a reach and touch for naming the natural world, would later help him offer the history of a world turning unnatural, intolerable,"[36] writes Felstiner, a world that would kill his parents in the concentration camps of World War II and that would ultimately lead him to suicide.

Fifty thousand years ago, even the Neanderthals buried their dead with flowers. We know this, says Russell, because traces of pollen were left behind, "ancient versions of blue hyacinth, yellow groundsel, knapweed, and yarrow." [37] An artist friend, who first told me about Mondrian's late flower paintings, found herself painting a series of what she called "sad flower paintings" after her mother died from breast cancer. A poet tells me that, in her daily meditations, she often visits her dead parents as plants and flowers. Her mother is a peace lily. Her father is a pussy willow. Because they have taken the image of plants, she can go to them in a less fraught way than in their human form. She can sit close; she can *attend* to them. The image of the flower, it seems, mediates: between lovers, between the sick and the healthy, between the dead and the alive, and for the human body.

The Korean poet, Ko Un, in the preface to his book of poems entitled *Flowers of a Moment*, writes of the flowers laid on graves: "I am convinced this heart-offering of flowers is the essence of poetry. Long before [poetry], people prayed with poetic hearts for their dead to be reborn in another world, a world of flowers, flowers representing the sorrow arising between presence and absence." [38] These "word-flowers" are the flowers of a moment in his title, an image for feeling that arises from the hearts of the grieving, and words, he says, that arise in his dreams:

> That flower
> seen as I went down
> —as I was coming up
> I couldn't see it. [39]

In this poem, we, as readers, don't know if the speaker is going down into sleep or down a mountain, whether the flower has died or been lost, picked, or forgotten, and yet in these few words we feel the loss of all things disappeared on our return over familiar terrain, an edge that seems able to straddle both memory and forgetfulness. Here, the ephemeral and eternal nature of flower or person floats, neither real nor ideal but transcending both, Mallarmé's "flower which is absent from all bouquets."

How can one flower ever be alone?
Look, over there
in that dry river bed
so very homely
that might be your love.[40]

Ko Un states that the poems in his book "arose" from the shadows of sleep the way colors arise from night at dawn, almost imperceptibly. He says, "My brief poems have their *roots* in my dreams"[41] (my italics). Thus, they are inexplicable. They drift as flowers drift over the surface of the real world, in between sleeping and waking. The question that begins this poem—is it rhetorical? We know that flowers sometimes are alone. We have found them, a stalk of lupine or larkspur, though more often than not, they grow in clusters or patches. But over there, in the dry river bed, is someone else; we don't know if it is another flower or a person or a snake. The poem has turned to face us; it suddenly addresses a *you*. Whatever is in the dry river bed—we assume a flower—*might be* our love. Does he mean that the flower might be someone we love, perhaps someone who has died, or is our love, our capacity for love, emblemized in this flower? Or is the *you* a flower he is addressing? The poem doesn't answer. The image is there and more-than-there, a cipher, meeting place and edge of an opening world. What do we make of it? We halt at this edge between abstraction and representation. We must go further, up to the edge and past it. Who is our love? Who is the flower?

## III

*The Flower as Soul*

Ah, rosebush, why do you endlessly sway, through long rains, with your double rose?
They are like two aging wasps that have yet to take flight.
I see them from my heart, for my eyes are closed.
My love above the flowers has left but wind and cloud.

—*René Char*[42]

For over thirty years I have seen plants when I close my eyes. They began appearing when I was in my twenties and weeding my first garden. I saw what I'd pulled for hours, sometimes days afterward. I thought they were after-images, ghosts of what I had killed "with my bare hands." But then, flowers also appeared, often when I was most happy, or often, too, unexpectedly, not linked to anything I had just seen. I feel their color rather than see it, though their shapes are distinctly here, if instantaneously here and then gone. They are not generic (as our feelings are not generic) but specific: lily, columbine, rose, hyacinth, sometimes simply leaves. Like Ko Un's poems, they seem to rise up from the soil of mind I must be carrying inside me. I began this essay in search of what they might mean.

The image takes root at the heart of the world, writes the poet Adonis in his book *Sufism and Surrealism*, "a real world deeply rooted at the heart of the world of appearances."[43] This world, which the Sufi mystics say lies between the sensory world and the ideal or divine world, is accessed by the creative imagination, whose door of perception is the image itself. "The significance of the image," Adonis writes, "does not lie in its visible surface but rather in the fact that it is a threshold to whatever meaning it has and a door that leads the spectator to what is behind it: the absent or the abstract, in its essence or nature,"[44] in other words, the invisible, the unknown. What is unique about the flower image is that it is both threshold for this experience and *form* of that experience. What I mean is that at the same time that it exists as a means to contemplation, it also mirrors, in its shape and colors and perhaps fragrance, a specific and age-old path that one might take from unseeing to seeing, from ignorance to revelation, an organic, even alchemical, path that is shared by many cultures that have attempted to come face to face with the soul.

"Flowers are allegories of consciousness," writes Novalis, in a fragment quoted in Shapiro's essay on Mondrian.[45] I recognize the allegory, the agreed upon parallel between our inner experience and the outer world of appearances: from deep below the surface of the earth, which is colorless, dark, secret, a seed sprouts and sends up a shoot that flowers into its own unique form in the same way that a thought or dream or awareness arises from ignorance into knowledge, from nothingness into presence. As it enters the light of consciousness, it takes shape. It moves into *our* world, petal upon petal, growing from a center that often becomes sunken or hidden, yet signals with stripe and color, luring birds and bees and other seekers. Yet if it is to move past allegory to symbol, as Corbin would define it, it must call to us and we must respond. It must persuade us to follow, like the bee or fly, down its corridors into our own centers. It must not reveal everything; it must leave something for us to find. As Mallarmé writes, it must employ "evocation, allusion, suggestion."

I think you are among the flowers
that spill from walls and urge
the hummingbirds to drink and drink
from their fantastic hair.
Each day I believe more firmly
in this life of yours among the brilliance
that thrusts and blooms on into the blue
foyer of the sun. In this way
I understand my own flowering
as your shadow left advisedly
against the noise of loneliness
which would otherwise be your absence.

—*Christopher Howell* [46]

The image takes root in us perhaps because it finds not its allegory, but its home in our being, our inner earth, in centers and colors that resonate with it, or in the meadows and streambeds that constitute what Corbin calls the "mystic geography" [47] of the soul. In the lines above, excerpted from Howell's "Another Letter to the Soul," the flower/soul addressed is a climbing one, perhaps a clematis, and it is precisely *drawn* from all the others who are growing into the "blue / foyer of the sun." In the act of distinguishing it, "in this way" of seeing it alone, separate, the speaker is able to understand his own flowering as a "shadow" or parallel process. Or the "way" is perhaps that of belief, by which I think he means creative imagination, of first believing the flower is his soul, and then practicing that belief each day until he sees it as such. Howell suggests, in his image of the luxuriant vine, that, though we cannot see our souls, we might act *as though* we saw them. "The poet therefore does not explain or make clear but rather, as al-Buhtari says, only provides a flash, whose indication is enough," writes Adonis. [48] Enough for what? Enough to confirm that there is in absence a promise of presence, that "an interior world exists, which is invisible, unknown and inaccessible by logical or rational means." [49]

This interior world varies person to person, moment by moment, because it is a process, not a product. In other words, it is creative. The mystery of any true image, regardless of whether it is flower or not, is that its meaning is not stable, but fluctuates. "Unchanging knowledge is unchanging ignorance," Adonis says, quoting the Sufi master al-Niffari. [50] The transitory and fugitive beauty of a flower is particularly suited as symbol of this fluctuation. What makes an image capable of engaging our active, not passive, imagination, Corbin says, is that a symbol "is never 'explained' once and for all, but must be deciphered over and over again."[51] We never tire of flowers. We never tire of great poems or paintings because they bring something new to us each time we encounter them, news which is created *in the act of perception itself.* The knowledge we glean from this act is new because it is created anew, in the moment of *inter*change between perceived and preceptor. Unlike allegory, wherein the image is interpreted within an agreed upon frame, this way of seeing posits an expanding, not limiting, view of perception, a chemical or, should we say, alchemical exchange.

"When a plant receives this kind of communication, it begins altering the wavelengths its chemicals reflect in order to offer itself to your imaginal sight, for you to gather it," we remember reading in Berssenbrugge's poem. She finishes her poem with these two stanzas:

> Through this method of your perception of its color, its fragrance, an infusion of
> its petals, you receive not only molecules of plant compound itself, but also the
> meaning in yourself that the plant was responding to.

> So, there is meaning in a chemical compound.[52]

Color, fragrance, "an infusion of its petals" travel from one body into another body, via the senses, and chemically alter that body, changing it from within, what we might describe as the physics of perception. The flower image centers us, and, if we are practicing a particular kind of creative imagination, centers inside us. We can feel that kind of center inside our own bodies, perhaps in our own minds, the way focus begins and then grows exponentially out. Growth as a kind of petalling. Consciousness as a flower act. A dahlia. A spider mum. A rose. The movement back and forth between exterior image and interior one is what constitutes the visionary experience. Our "imaginal" or interior awareness of an image directly stimulates our psyche and we, in turn, urge more of the image to reveal itself, a perpetual movement toward shared meaning, what we might call the metaphysics of perception.

The language of flowers, which is said to have originated in ancient Persia, and which devolved in Victorian England and Europe into a sentimental system of associations between specific plants and specific human feelings such as fidelity, sympathy, friendship, is, according to Corbin, a system of symbols that offered "unlimited possibilities to liturgical imagination as well as for rituals of meditation." The flowers "evoke psychic reactions, which transmute the forms contemplated into energies corresponding to them," he writes in his book *Celestial Body, Spiritual Earth*.[53] The flower, in being seen, lights up or wakes up or enables us to see the flower in us, to see our own beauty, as it were, something we instinctively love. The form of the flower leads us to the experience of beauty, not the appreciation of it. It lures us, as it does the bee, into pollinating or quickening ourselves.

And where does this alchemy take place? If it is possible to speak of place when describing the processes of the imagination, it must be inside us. The Sufis located it in the heart, as Jalaluddin Rumi writes, in this translation by Corbin:

> Before the apparition of a superhuman beauty,
> Before this Form which flowers from the ground like a
> rose before her,
> Like an Image raising its head from the secrecy of the
> heart [54]

The image, which attracts us with its intimation of something *more* than us, flowers from the earth, like a rose but not a rose, something that takes form in order for us to see it. Like the penumbra of light around a tree at dusk, it is both tree and not tree. At the same time, it is "like" something rising inside us. Char says of the double roses, "I see them from the heart, for my eyes are closed." Berssenbrugge writes, "Even with closed eyes, I see flowers in the center of my sight." To see with one's eyes closed is to see oneself as a place of apparition, to inhabit the geography of the imagination. The flower serves as a mandala, offering endless passageways into this geography, a land that cannot be mapped because it is endless, though we can be sure that there are meadows in the vast realms established there.

It is this geography that Robert Duncan refers to in one of his most celebrated poems. Though the scene appears to him at first as if it were imaginary, he makes clear that it is rather an *imaginal* one, one that is created inside the body, located "near the heart," and thus real. The poem's lines begin with the title "Often I am Permitted to Return to a Meadow":

> as if it were a scene made-up by the mind,
> that is not mine, but is a made place,
>
> that is mine, it is so near to the heart,
> an eternal pasture folded in all thought

so that there is a hall therein
that is a made place, created by light
wherefrom the shadows that are forms fall.[55]

The "eternal pasture folded in all thought" of which Duncan speaks has its twin in the real meadows and gardens we walk through and the bouquets we hold in our hands. Mid-summer, the flowers, large as soup bowls, small as thimbles of blown glass, their stamens chalky with purple-black pollen caking onto the petals, are the dominant species in the world. "The notion that spirit might turn out in some sense to be matter (and plant matter, no less!) is a threat to our sense of separateness and godliness. Spiritual knowledge comes from above or within, but surely not from plants. Christians have a name for someone who believes otherwise—pagan," writes Michael Pollan in his book *The Botany of Desire*.[56] The forms of flowers are perhaps the most perfect forms because we recognize in them forces that are already inherent in us. Perhaps this is the knowledge that drew Morris Graves, after his many attempts to depict the inner world through abstractions, to paint his winter still lives and summer bouquets, and why we, in turn, are drawn to them.

## Introduction

1. William Blake, *Selected Poetry and Prose* (New York: Modern Library, 1953), 123.

2. Neil Roberts, *A Companion to Twentieth Century Poetry* (Hoboken: Wiley-Blackwell, 2003), 135.

3. Ezra Pound, *Literary Essays of Ezra Pound* (New York: New Directions, 1935), 4.

4. John Berger, *Ways of Seeing* (London: British Broadcasting Corporation/Penguin Books, 1972), 9-10.

5. M.H. Abrams, *Natural Supernaturalism: Tradition and Revolution in Romantic Literature* (New York: W.W. Norton & Company, 1971), 277.

6. Ibid., 418

7. Ezra Pound, "Vorticism," *The Fortnightly Review* 571 (1914): 465-67.

8. Novalis, *Notes for a Romantic Encyclopaedia / Das Allemeine Brouillon,* David W. Wood, trans. (Albany, NY: State University of New York Press, 2007).

9. Pound, *The Cantos of Ezra Pound.* (New York: New Directions, 1993), 816.

10. Novalis, *Pollen and Fragments: Selected Poetry and Prose of Novalis,* Arthur Versluis, trans. (Grand Rapids, MI: Phanes Press, 1989).

11. T.S. Eliot, *The Waste Land and Other Poems* (New York: Signet, 1998), 51.

12. H.D. *Tribute to Freud* (New York: New Directions, 1984), 35.

13. Abrams, 155.

14. Pound, *The Cantos,* 817.

15. Susan Sontag, *At the Same Time: Essays and Speeches* (New York: Farrar Straus Giroux, 2007), 124.

16. André Breton, *Manifestoes of Surrealism,* Richard Seaver and Helen R. Lane, trans. (Ann Arbor: The University of Michigan Press, 1972), 136.

17. Joron, 25.

18. Federico García Lorca, "Theory and Function of the *Duende*" in *Toward the Open Field: Poets on the Art of Poetry 1800-1950,* Melissa Kwasny, ed. (Middletown, CT: Wesleyan University Press, 2004), 198.

19. Ibid.

20. Pablo Neruda, "The Lamb and the Pinecone" in *Neruda and Vallejo: Selected Poems*, Robert Bly, ed. (Boston: Beacon Press, 1971), 158.

21. René Char. "Argument," translated by Robert Baker, personal correspondence, 2012.

22. Char, *Hypnos Waking,* William Matthews, ed. (New York: Random House, 1956), 109.

23. Nancy Kline Piore, *Lightning: The Poetry of René Char* (Boston: Northeastern University Press, 1981), xvi.

24. Adonis. *An Introduction to Arab Poetics*, Catherine Cobham, trans. (Austin: University of Texas Press, 1990), 73.

25. Adonis. *Sufism and Surrealism,* Judith Bumberbatch, trans. (London: SAQI, 2005), 38.

26. Tom Cheetham, *Green Man, Earth Angel: The Prophetic Tradition and the Battle for the Soul of the World* (Albany: State University of New York Press, 2005), 34.

27. Ibid, 66.

## *Learning to Speak with Them*

1. Stephané Mallarmé, "Crisis in Poetry" in *Mallarmé: Selected Prose Poems, Essays, & Letters* (Baltimore: John Hopkins Press, 1956), 40.
2. A. Day Grove, ed., *The Sky Clears: Poetry of the American Indians*, Frances Densmore, trans. (Lincoln: University of Nebraska Press, 1951.)
3. Ibid.
4. Frank B. Linderman, *Pretty-Shield: Medicine Woman of the Crows* (Lincoln: University of Nebraska Press, 1972), 126.
5. André Breton, "Second Manifesto of Surrealism" in *Manifestoes of Surrealism*, Richard Seaver and Helen R. Lane, trans. (Ann Arbor: University of Michigan Press, 1972), 158.
6. Joseph Epes Brown, *The Sacred Pipe: Black Elk's Account of the Seven Rites of the Oglala Sioux* (Norman: University of Oklahoma Press, 1953), 58.
7. H.D. *Collected Poems: 1912-1944* (New York: New Directions, 1983), 55.
8. George Oppen, "An Adequate Vision: From the Daybooks," *Ironwood* (1982), 9.
9. Henri Corbin, *Creative Imagination in the Sufism of Ibn Arabi* (Princeton: Princeton University Press, 1981), 247.
10. Ralph Waldo Emerson, "The Poet," in *The Selected Writings of Ralph Waldo Emerson* (New York: Modern Library, 1992), 298.
11. H.D. *Notes on Thought and Vision* (San Francisco: City Lights, 1982), 20.
12. Adelaide Morris, "The Concept of Projection: H.D.'s Visionary Powers," in *Signets*, Rachel Blau DuPlessis and Susan Friedman, eds. (Madison: University of Wisconsin Press, 1981), 282.
13. Corbin, *Creative Imagination*, 264.
14. Henri Corbin, *The Man of Light in Iranian Sufism* (New Lebanon, New York: Omega Publications, 1994), 16.
15. Corbin, *Creative Imagination*, 217.
16. H.D. *Collected Poems*, 5.
17. Pound, 12.
18. Louise Glück, *The Wild Iris* (Hopewell: Ecco Press, 1993), 1.
19. Clayton Eshleman, *Juniper Fuse: Upper Paleothic Imagination and the Construction of the Underworld* (Middletown: Wesleyan University Press, 2003), xxii.
20. Pound, 26.
21. Charles Baudelaire, *Selected Poems*, Wallace Fowlie, trans. (New York: Dover, 2012), 5.
22. Alex Preminger and T.V.F. Brogan, eds., *The New Princeton Encyclopedia of Poetry and Poetics* (Princeton: Princeton University Press, 1999), 1256.
23. Mallarmé, 40.
24. Preminger and Brogan, 1256.
25. Corbin, *Creative Imagination*, 236.
26. Mallarmé, 42.
27. George Oppen, *The Collected Poems of George Oppen* (New York: New Directions, 1975), 78.
28. George Oppen, "George Oppen's Working Papers," Stephen Cope, ed. *The Germ*, 4. Santa Cruz. The Poetic Research Bloc (May 1999).
29. Oppen. *Collected*, 54.
30. Emerson, 298.

## Conference of the Birds

1. Jonathan Trouen-Trend, *Birding Babylon: A Soldier's Journal from Iraq* (San Francisco: Sierra Club, 2006), 10.
2. John Seabrook, "Back from Iraq: Birds of America," Talk of the Town, *New Yorker* 24 April, 2006, 52.
3. Farid ud-Din Attar, *The Conference of the Birds*, Mantiq Ut-Tair, trans. (Shambhala: Berkeley, 1971), 9.
4. Farid ud-Din Attar, *The Conference of the Birds*, Afkham Darbandi and Dick Davis, trans. (New York: Penguin Books, 1984).
5. Attar. *The Conference*, Ut-Tair, 9.
6. Ibid., 20.
7. Ibid., 27.
8. Ibis., 25.
9. Preminger, Alex and T.V.F. Brogan, eds., *The New Princeton Encyclopedia of Poetry and Poetics* (Princeton: Princeton University Press, 1999), 32.
10. Ibid.
11. Bruno Snell, *The Discovery of Mind in Greek Philosophy and Literature*, T. G. Rosenmeyer, trans. (New York: Dover, 1953), 200-201.
12. Preminger and Brogan, 32.
13. Attar, *The Conference*, Darbandi and Davis, 16.
14. Attar, *The Conference*, Ut-Tair, 8.
15. Ovid, *The Metamorphosis*, Rolfe Humphries, trans. (Bloomington: Indiana University Press, 1955), 151.
16. Seabrook, 52.
17. Kenneth I. Helphand, *Defiant Gardens: Making Gardens in Wartime* (San Antonio: Trinity University Press, 2006), 34.
18. Jessica Adley and Andrea Grant, "The Environmental Consequences of War," Sierra Club of Canada. 17 May 2006. <www.sierraclub.ca/national/postings/war-and-environment.html>.
19. Solana Pyne, "Leaving a Mess in Mesopotamia: Long-term Damage from a Short-term War," *Village Voice* 16-22 Apr. 2003. 17 May 2006.
20. Montana Human Rights Network, *Drumming Up Resentment: The Anti-Indian Movement in Montana*, Helena, Montana, 2000.
21. Edwin Dobb, "Pennies from Hell," *Harper's Magazine* Oct. (1996), 39+. *Infotrac*. 28 Mar. 2007.
22. Ibid.
23. Scott Weidensaul, *Living on the Wind: Across the Hemisphere with Migratory Birds* (New York: North Point, 1999), 243.
24. Ibid., 185.
25. Ibid., 339.

## Windswept

1. Rebecca Solnit, *As Eve Said To the Serpent: On Landscape, Gender, and Art* (Athens: The University of Georgia Press, 2001), 163.
2. Linder, Traci. Interview. Holter Museum of Art, Helena, Montana, May 2009.
3. Solnit, 161.
4. René Char. *The Word as Archipelago,* Robert Baker, trans. (Oakland: Omnidawn, 2012).
5. Linder.
6. Ibid.
7. Ibid.
8. Ibid.
9. Ibid.
10. Solnit, 163.
11. Linder.
12. Ibid.

## Women and Nature

1. Bill Nye, interview, *Campbell Brown.* CNN. 8 Oct. 2000 <http://archives.cnn.com TRANSCRIPTS/0910/08/ec.01.html>
2. Susan Griffin, *Woman and Nature: The Roaring Inside Her* (New York: Harper and Row, 1978), xv.
3. Ezra Pound, *Literary Essays of Ezra Pound* (New York: New Directions, 1935), 45.
4. Susan Griffin, "Thoughts on Writing: A Diary" in *The Writer on Her Work,* Janet Sternburg, ed. (New York: Norton, 1980), 110.
5. Ibid., 114.
6. Griffin, *Women and Nature*, xv.
7. Elizabeth Willis, *Meteoric Flowers* (Middletown, CT: Wesleyan University Press, 2006), 28.
8. Ibid., 46.
9. Henry Corbin, *Spiritual Body, Celestial Earth* (Princeton: Princeton University Press, 1989), 5.
10. Tom Cheetham, *Green Man, Earth Angel: The Prophetic Tradition and the Battle for the Soul of the World* (Albany: State University of New York Press, 2005), 110.
11. Gaston Bachelard, *The Poetics of Space,* Maria Jolas, trans. (Boston: Beacon Press, 1994), 100.
12. Adonis. *Sufism and Surrealism,* Judith Cumberbatch, trans. (London: Saqi, 2005), 121.
13. Leslie Scalapino, "Leslie Scalapino asks Mei-Mei Berssenbrugge about Communicating with Plants" in *War and Peace: Vision and Text.* (Oakland: O Books, 2009), 58.
14. Ibid., 63.
15. Ibid., 61.
16. Mei-Mei Berssenbrugge, "Glitter," *Conjunctions* 54: (2010), 254.
17. Maurice Merleau-Ponty, *The Merleau-Ponty Aesthetic Reader: Philosophy and Painting,* Galen Johnson and Michael B. Smith, eds. (Evanston, IL: Northwestern University Press, 1994), 124.
18. Ibid.
19. Brenda Hillman, *Practical Water* (Middletown, CT: Wesleyan University Press, 2009), 33.
20. Ibid., 48.
21. Ibid., 34.

22. Ibid., 4.

23. Ibid., 51.

24. Janice N. Harrington, "The Body and Embodiment of Earth: Reclaiming, Reimagining, and Recognizing the Other in the Poetry of Susan Griffin and Lucille Clifton." AWP Conference, Denver. 8 Apr. 2010.

25. Lucille Clifton, "the earth is a living thing" in *Black Nature: Four Centuries of African American Nature Poetry,* Camille T. Dungy, ed. (Athens, GA: University of Georgia Press, 2009), 6.

26. Adonis, 120.

27. Leslie Marmon Silko, "Chapulin's Portrait," *The Kenyon Review* Winter 2010, 113.

28. Susan Griffin, *The Eros of Everyday Life: Essays on Ecology, Gender and Society* (New York: Doubleday, 1995), 7.

29. Mary Daly, interview with Susan Bridle, *Enlighten Next Magazine* Fall/Winter (1999).

30. Griffin, *Eros*, 39.

## God-Step at the Margins of Thought

1. Robert Duncan, "The Truth and Life of Myth" in *Fictive Certainties* (New York: New Directions, 1985), 3.

2. Robert Duncan, *The Opening of the Field* (New York: New Directions, 1960), 62.

3. Aaron Parrett, "Ezra Pound's Philosophy of Harmony." Unpublished essay.

4. H.D. *Hermetic Definition* (New York: New Directions, 1972).

5. Christopher Howell, *Though Silence: The Ling Wei Texts* (Sandpoint, ID: Lost Horse Press, 1999).

6. Kamau Brathwaite, *Born to Slow Horses* (Middletown, CT: Wesleyan University Press, 2005).

7. H.D., *Helen in Egypt* (New York: New Directions, 1961), 87.

8. H.D., *Tribute to Freud* (New York: New Directions, 1984), 44.

9. Ibid., 45.

10. Ibid., 48.

11. Adelaide Morris, "The Concept of Projection: H.D., Modernism and the Psychoanalysis of Seeing" in *Signets,* Rachel Blau DuPlessis and Susan Friedman, eds. (Madison: University of Wisconsin Press, 1990), 277.

12. Ezra Pound, "How to Read" in *Literary Essays of Ezra Pound* (New York: New Directions, 1935), 25.

13. H.D., *Collected Poems 1912-1944* (New York: New Directions, 1982), 517.

14. Ibid., 521.

15. Robert Pogue Harrison, *The Dominion of the Dead* (Chicago: The University of Chicago Press, 2003), x.

16. Joyelle McSweeney, "Poetics, Revelations, and Catastrophes: an Interview with Kamau Brathwaite," *Rain Taxi Online Edition*, Fall 2005.

17. Henry Corbin, *Avicenna and the Visionary Recital,* Willard R. Trask, trans. (New York: Pantheon, 1960), 260.

18. Harrison, 30.

19. Ibid., ix-x.

20. Ibid., 28.

21. Henry Corbin, *Spiritual Body and Celestial Earth* (Princeton: Princeton University Press, 1989), 5.

## Dov'è il Tevere

1. Rainer Maria Rilke, *Rilke and Andreas-Salomé: A Love Story in Letters* (New York: Norton, 2006), 81.
2. Ibid.
3. Victoria Finlay, *Color: A Natural History of the Palette* (New York: Random House, 2004), 72.
4. Rebecca Solnit, *Field Guide to Getting Lost* (New York: Penguin, 2006), 180.
5. Rilke, 89.
6. Robert Pogue Harrison, *Gardens: An Essay on the Human Condition* (Chicago: The University of Chicago Press, 2008), 116.
7. Rilke, 78.
8. Harrison, 57.
9. Rilke, 73.
10. Ibid., 93.
11. Ibid., 88.
12. Harrison, 118.
13. Ibid., 20.
14. Ibid.
15. Ibid.

## The Imaginal Book of Cave Paintings

1. Piers Vitebsky, *The Reindeer People: Living with Animals and Spirits in Siberia* (Boston: Houghton Mifflin, 2005), 7.
2. Mavis Ann Loscheider Greer, *Archaeological Analysis of Rock Art Sites in the Smith River Drainage of Central Montana.* Dissertation. Graduate School, University of Missouri-Columbia. December 1995, 69.
3. Ibid., 69.
4. James D. Keyser and Michael A. Klassen, *Plains Indian Rock Art* (Seattle: University of British Columbia Press, 2001), 46.
5. David Lewis-Williams, *The Mind in the Cave* (London: Thames and Hudson, 2002), illus. 6.
6. David S. Whitely, *The Art of the Shaman: Rock Art of California* (Salt Lake: University of Utah, 2000), 44.
7. Greer, 69.
8. Greer, 68.
9. Keyser and Klassen, 164.
10. Clayton Eschleman, *Juniper Fuse: Upper Paleolithic Imagination & the Construction of the Underworld* (Middletown, CT: Wesleyan University Press, 2003), xiv.
11. Sara Scott, "Early Art," *Montana Magazine.* July/August 2007, 72.
12. Victoria Finlay, *Color: A Natural History of the Palette* (New York: Random House, 2004), 26.
13. Sara A. Scott, Dr. James D. Keyser and Dr. Johannes H.N. Loubser, "The Hellgate Pictographs: Shamanism and Ritual in West-Central Montana, *Archaeology in Montana* 41.1 (2000), 49.
14. Scott, 72.
15. Keyser and Klassen, 8.
16. Lewis-Williams, 192.

17. John Berger, "The Chauvet Cave" in *The Shape of a Pocket* (New York: Pantheon Books, 2001), 41.
18. Sara A Scott, et al., "AMS Dates from Four Late Prehistoric Period Rock Art Sites in West Central Montana," *Plains Anthropologist* 50.193 (2005), 57.
19. Scott, Keyser, and Loubser, 44.
20. Robert Pogue Harrison, *The Dominion of the Dead* (Chicago: University of Chicago Press, 2003), xi.
21. Ibid., 30.
22. Ibid., 44.
23. Michael W. Taylor, James D. Keyser, and Phillip Cash Cash, "The Roles of Women in Columbia Plateau Rock Art," in *American Indian Rock Art: Volume 34* (Tucson: AIRA Research Association, 2008), 133.
24. Ibid., 134.
25. Keyser and Klassen, 219.
26. Henry Corbin, *Spiritual Body and Celestial Earth* (Princeton: Princeton University Press, 1989), 25.
27. Henry Corbin, *Avicenna and the Visionary Recital* (Princeton: Princeton University Press, 1990), 85.
28. Harrison, 50.
29. Whitely, 30.
30. Keyser and Klassen, 28.
31. Ibid., 219.
32. Lewis-Williams, 178.
33. Florian Ebeling, *The Secret History of Hermes Trismegistus: Hermeticism from Ancient to Modern Times* (Ithaca: Cornell University Press, 2007), ix.
34. Ibid., 132.
35. Gaston Bachelard, *The Poetics of Space*, Maria Jolas, trans. (Boston: Beacon Press, 1994), 218.
36. Ibid., 152.
37. Ibid., 222.
38. Mircea Eliade, *Shamanism: Archaic Techniques of Ecstasy* (London: Arkana, 1989), 91.
39. Berger, 37.
40. Robert Pogue Harrison, *Forests: The Shadow of Civilization* (Chicago: University of Chicago Press, 1992), 4.
41. Lewis-Williams, 149.
42. Harrison, 4.
43. Maurice Merleau-Ponty, "Eye and Mind," in *The Merleau-Ponty Aesthetics Reader: Philosophy and Painting* (Evanston, IL: Northwestern University Press, 1993), 126.
44. Lewis-Williams, 51
45. Ibid., 88.
46. Alexander Marshak, *The Roots of Civilization: The Cognitive Beginnings of Man's First Art, Symbol and Notation* (New York: McGraw Hill, 1972), 276.
47. Lewis-Williams, 127.
48. Ibid., 129.
49. Ibid., 130.
50. Ibid.
51. Keyser and Klassen, 113.
52. Jerome Rothenberg, ed., *Technicians of the Sacred: A Range of Poetries from Africa, America, Asia & Oceania* 5 (New York: Anchor, 1969).

53. Lewis-Williams, 93.

54. Keyser and Klassen, 112.

55. James Hillman, *The Dream and the Underworld* (New York: Harper and Row, 1979), 51.

56. Eschleman, 54.

57. Lewis-Williams, 209.

58. Keyser and Klassen, 168-9.

59. Hillman, 45.

60. Lewis-Williams,169.

61. Eschleman, xvi.

62. Eschleman, 47.

63. Jerome Rothenberg and Jeffrey C. Robinson, eds., *Poems for the Millennium, Volume Three* (Berkeley: University of California Press, 2009), 190.

64. Erwin Rohde, *Psyche: The Cult of Souls and Belief in Immortality among the Greeks,* W.B. Hillis, trans. (Eugene: Wipf & Stock Publishers, 2006), Chapter VIII.

65. Eliade, xix.

66. Ibid., 96.

67. Ibid., 136.

68. Lewis-Williams, 223.

69. Eliade, 93.

70. Eliade, 94.

71. Robert Calasso, *Literature and the Gods* (New York: Knopf, 2001), 146.

72. Harrison, *Forests,* 33.

73. Lewis-Williams, 134.

74. Harrison, *Forests,* 45.

75. Piers Vitebsky, *The Reindeer People: Living with Animals and Spirits in Siberia* (Boston: Houghton Mifflin, 2005), 234.

76. Ibid. 230.

77. Eliade, 509.

78. Ibid.

79. Eschleman, 43.

80. Adonis, *Sufism and Surrealism,* Judith Cumberbatch, trans. (London: Saqi, 2005), 19.

81. Hillman, 55.

82. Corbin, *Avicenna,* 164.

83. Ibid., 194.

84. Eliade, 510.

85. Rothenberg and Robinson, 29.

86. Finlay, 67.

### The Flower Artist

1. Theodore F. Wolff, *Morris Graves: Flower Paintings* (Seattle: University of Washington Press, 1994), n.p.

2. Ibid. n.p.

3. Robert Gordon and Andrew Forge, *The Last Flowers of Manet,* Richard Howard, trans. (New York: Abradale Press/Abrams, 1999), 14.

4. David Shapiro in *Mondrian: Flowers* (New York: Harry N. Abrams, 1991, 13.

5. Alexander Marshak, *The Roots of Civilization: The Cognitive Beginnings of Man's First Art, Symbol and Notation* (New York: McGraw Hill, 1972).

6. Ranier Maria Rilke, *The Selected Poetry of Rainer Maria Rilke,* Stephen Mitchell, trans. (New York: Vintage, 1984), 75.

7. Louisiana Museum of Modern Art, *The Flower as Image* (LMMA: Humlebaek, Denmark, 2004), 5.

8. Charles Baudelaire, *The Painter of Modern Life and Other Essays,* Jonathan Mayne, trans. (New York: Da Capo, 1984), 13.

9. Ibid.

10. Gaston Bachelard, *The Poetics of Space,* Maria Jolas, trans. (Boston: Beacon Press, 1994), 187.

11. Wolff, n.p.

12. Stephané Mallarmé, "Crisis in Poetry" in *Mallarmé: Selected Prose Poems, Essays, & Letters* (Baltimore: John Hopkins Press, 1956), 41.

13. Ibid.

14. Wolff, n.p.

15. Ibid.

16. Mondrian, 18.

17. Pablo Neruda, *Book of Questions,* William O'Daly, trans. (Port Townsend: Copper Canyon, 2001), 3.

18. William Blake, "The Sick Rose" in *The Norton Anthology of Poetry,* Fourth Edition, Margaret Ferguson, Mary Jo Salter, and Jon Stallworthy, eds. (New York: W.W. Norton & Company, 1996), 680.

19. Henry Corbin, *Alone with the Alone: Creative Imagination in the Sufism of Ibn 'Arabi* (Princeton, NY: Princeton University Press, 1969), 14.

20. Ibid.

21. Sharman Apt Russell, *Anatomy of a Rose* (Cambridge: Perseus, 2001), 9.

22. Peter Thompkins and Christopher Bird, *The Secret Life of Plants* (New York: Harper, 1989), 117.

23. Mondrian, 10.

24. Russell, 6.

25. Mondrian, 29.

26. Ibid., 24.

27. Russell, 49.

28. Novalis, *Notes for a Romantic Encyclopaedia: Das Allgemeine Brouillon,* David W. Wood, trans. (Albany, New York: SUNY Press, 2007), 13.

29. Judith Goldman and Leslie Scalapino, eds., "Mei-Mei Berssenbrugge and Leslie Scalapino" in *War and Peace: Vision and Text* (Oakland: O Books, 2009), 58.

30. Ibid., 62-63.

31. Thompkins and Bird, 112.

32. Goldman and Scalapino, 63.

33. Ibid.

34. John Felstiner, "Deep in the time-crevasse," *Parthenon West Review,* 4 (2006).

35. Ibid.

36. Ibid.

37. Russell, 99.

38. Ko Un, *Flowers of the Moment,* Brother Anthony, Young-moo Kim and Gary Gach, trans. (Rochester, New York: Boa Editions), 2006, 11.

39. Ibid., 46.

40. Ibid., 39.

41. Ibid.,12.

42. René Char, *The Word as Archipelago,* Robert Baker, trans. (Oakland: Omnidawn, 2012), n.p.

43. Adonis, *Sufism and Surrealism,* Judith Cumberbatch, trans. (London: Saqi, 2005), 138.

44. Ibid., 171.

45. Mondrian, 9.

46. Christopher Howell, *Dreamless and Possible: Poems New and Selected* (Seattle: University of Washington Press, 2010), 6.

47. Corbin, 218.

48. Adonis, 133.

49. Ibid., 12.

50. Ibid., 29.

51. Corbin, 14.

52. Goldman and Scalapino, 63.

53. Henry Corbin, *Spiritual Body, Celestial Earth* (Princeton, NJ: Princeton University Press, 1989), 31.

54. Corbin, *Alone with the Alone,* 171.

55. Robert Duncan, *The Opening of the Field* (New York: New Directions, 1973), 7.

56. Michael Pollan, *The Botany of Desire: A Plant's-Eye View of the World* (New York: Random House, 2002), 172.

Melissa Kwasny is author of four collections of poems, including *The Nine Senses* (Milkweed Editions, 2011) and *Thistle* (Lost Horse Press, 2006), winner of the Idaho Prize for Poetry. She is also editor of the celebrated anthology, *Toward the Open Field: Poets on the Art of Poetry 1800-1950* (Wesleyan University Press), and co-editor (with M.L. Smoker) of *I Go to the Ruined Place: Contemporary Poems in Defense of Global Human Rights* (Lost Horse Press). Her poems and essays have appeared in *Crazyhorse, Field, Michigan Quarterly Review, American Poetry Review, Kenyon Review, Antioch Review, Gettysburg Review, Pleiades,* and many other journals. She lives in the mountains near Helena, Montana.